IRIS
Folding
COMPENDIUM

D1337384

IRIS
Folding
COMPENDIUM

INCLUDING 3 NEW PATTERNS

**Maruscha Gaasenbeek
and Tine Beauveser**

FORTE PUBLISHERS

© 2003 Forte Uitgevers, Utrecht
© 2003 for the translation by the publisher
Original title: *Basisboek IRISvouwen®*

Fourth printing May 2004

ISBN 90 5877 278 0
NUR 475

This is a publication from
Forte Uitgevers BV
P.O. Box 1394
3500 BJ Utrecht
The Netherlands

For more information about the creative books
available from Forte Uitgevers:
www.hobby-party.com

Publisher: Els Neele
Editor: Stella Ruhe
Photography and digital image editing:
Fotografie Gerhard Witteveen, Apeldoorn,
the Netherlands
Cover and inner design: Bade creatieve
communicatie, Baarn, the Netherlands

Contents

Preface

Everybody likes to receive post. Particularly greetings cards, because that shows somebody was thinking of you. And it is even better if the card is home-made! You may well say that you have to be able to make greetings cards. Well, with IRIS folding, you can. IRIS folding is the new way of making cards which everybody can do. The material you need is free, because all the cards in this book have been made from the inside of used envelopes. Look at the post you receive each day, from your bank, your insurance company or your children's school and take a look at the print on the inside of the envelopes. You will find the most attractive colours and patterns and envelopes are, therefore, worth collecting. You cut the paper into strips and use it to enclose the hole in the centre of the card, just like the iris of the eye encloses the pupil. The final result is always surprisingly attractive, because you in fact work on the back of the card. Your choice of paper and the combination of strips make each card original and creative.

Apart from all the templates used in *IRIS Folding with Envelopes, Festive IRIS Folding* and *IRIS Folding for Christmas*, this excellent book uses three extra templates. They are the cooking pear, the cherries and the shell, all of which are filled with strips in a surprising way.
Use the clear explanations given in this book to discover the many possibilities the templates have to offer. You will really enjoy yourself making IRIS folding cards!

Have fun!

Maruscha *Tine*

Techniques

The starting point for IRIS folding is the pattern. Cut the outer shape of the pattern out of the card and then fill the hole from the outside to the inside with folded strips of used envelopes. You will be working on the reverse side of your card, so in fact you will be working on a mirror image; when you have finished, you stick it onto another card. For a round pattern, select four different envelopes where the patterns and colours combine and contrast nicely. Cut all the envelopes into strips in the same way, for example, from left to right. The number of strips you will need depends on the pattern; you will need between four and eight strips. The width of the strips also depends on the pattern and is stated for each card. First, you need to fold the edge of the strips over and sort them into each different type of envelope. Next, you cover each section in turn by following the numbers (1, 2, 3, 4, 5, etc), so that you rotate the design.
Lay the strips with the fold facing towards the middle of the pattern and then stick them on the left-hand and right-hand sides of the card using adhesive tape. Finally, use an attractive piece of deco tape to cover the hole in the middle. Avoid colour differences by using one envelope for the same design.

The basic triangle, the basic circle and the basic square
The most important thing is to start with the basic triangle, the basic circle and the basic square because from this, you will learn the unique folding and sticking technique needed for all the patterns.

Start at the beginning. You will notice that you quickly get used to the technique of IRIS folding.

Preparation
The basic triangle
1. Take a white card (14.8 x 21 cm). Fold it double and lay it down with the inside facing towards you.
2. Draw pencil lines on the left-hand side of the card halfway along the width and length. These lines will help you determine the place for your pattern.
3. Copy the basic triangle pattern 1A from this book.
4. Place this model on the left-hand side of the card on the lines which you drew earlier.
5. Use a pin to prick through the pattern and the card in the three corners of the pattern.
6. Remove the pattern and carefully cut the triangle out of the card. Tape the basic triangle pattern (page 12) to your cutting mat.
7. Place the card on top with the hole exactly over the pattern (you should be looking at the back of the card) and stick the left-hand side to your cutting mat using a couple of pieces of masking tape.
8. Choose three envelopes with different patterns.
9. Cut 2 cm wide strips from these envelopes (either lengthways or widthways) and make separate piles of colour A, colour B and colour C.
10. For each strip, fold a border (approximately 7 mm) along the entire length with the nice side facing outwards.

The basic circle

1. Lay the card (13.2 x 9.3 cm) down with the back facing towards you.
2. Draw two pencil lines through the middle of the card. These lines will help you determine the place for your pattern.
3. Adjust the circle cutter to Ø 6 cm.
4. Place the circle cutter on the cross point of the two pencil lines on your card and cut the circle out.
5. Copy the basic circle pattern 1 from this book and tape it to your cutting mat.
6. Place the card on top with the hole exactly over the pattern (you should be looking at the back of the card) and stick the left-hand side to your cutting mat using a couple of pieces of masking tape.
7. Choose four envelopes with different patterns.
8. Cut 2 cm wide strips from these envelopes (either lengthways or widthways) and make separate piles of colour A, colour B, colour C and colour D.
9. For each strip, fold a border (approximately 7 mm) along the entire length with the nice side facing outwards.

The basic square

1. Lay the card (13.8 x 9.5 cm) down with the back facing towards you.
2. Draw two pencil lines through the middle of the card. These lines will help you determine the place for your pattern.
3. Copy the basic square pattern 1 from this book.

4. Place this model on the card using the lines which you drew earlier.
5. Use a pin to prick through the pattern and the card in the four corners. Remove the pattern and carefully cut the square out of the card.
6. Tape the basic square pattern 1 to your cutting mat.
7. Place the card on top with the hole exactly over the pattern (you should be looking at the back of the card) and stick the top and bottom edges to your cutting mat using a couple of pieces of masking tape.
8. Choose four envelopes with different patterns.
9. Cut 2 cm wide strips from these envelopes (either lengthways or widthways) and make separate piles of colour A, colour B, colour C and colour D.
10. For each strip, fold a border (approximately 7 mm) along the entire length with the nice side facing outwards.

IRIS folding
The triangle

1. Take a folded strip of colour A and place this over section 1 of the pattern with the folded side facing towards the middle. Allow 1 cm to stick out on the left-hand and right-hand sides and cut off the rest.
2. Stick the strip to the card on the left-hand and right-hand sides using a small piece of adhesive tape, but remain at least 0.5 cm from the side of the card.

3. Take a strip of colour B and place it on section 2 of the pattern. Also tape this to the left-hand and right-hand sides of the card.
4. Take a strip of colour C. Place this on section 3 and stick it into place.
5. You have now gone all the way around. Start again with colour A on section 4, colour B on section 5 and colour C on section 6.

Continue going around the card. The strips on sections 1, 4, 7, 10 and 13 of this pattern are all of colour A. The

strips on sections 2, 5, 8, 11 and 14 are all of colour B. The strips on sections 3, 6, 9, 12 and 15 are all of colour C.

The circle and the square
1. Take a folded strip of colour A and place this over section 1, exactly against the line of the pattern with the folded side facing towards the middle. Allow 0.5 cm to stick out on the left-hand and right-hand sides and cut the rest off. By doing so, the strip will also slightly stick out over the edge of the pattern at the bottom, so that section 1 is totally covered.
2. Stick it to the card on the left-hand and right-hand sides using a small piece of adhesive tape, but remain 0.5 cm from the side of the card.
3. Take a strip of colour B and place it on section 2 on the pattern. Tape this to the left-hand and right-hand sides of the card.
4. Take a strip of colour C. Place this on section 3 and stick it into place.
5. Take a strip of colour D. Place this on section 4 and stick it into place.
6. You have now gone all the way around. Start again with colour A on section 5, colour B on section 6, colour C on section 7 and colour D on section 8.

The strips on sections 1, 5, 9, 13, 17 and 21 of this pattern are all of colour A. The strips on sections 2, 6, 10, 14, 18 and 22 are all of colour B. The strips on sections 3, 7, 11, 15, 19 and 23 are all of colour C.

The strips on sections 4, 8, 12, 16, 20 and 24 are all of colour D.

Finishing

After section 15 (triangle) or 24 (circle and square), carefully remove the card and look at what you have made. Stick a single piece of holographic paper or deco tape in the middle on the back of the card. You can use punches, figure scissors, embossing stencils, etc. to finish the card. Stick small pieces of double-sided adhesive tape along the borders. Remove the protective layer and fix your design on a double card. Do not use glue, because all the paper strips place pressure on the card.

Cutting decorative borders

To cut the card using figure scissors, a pencil line is drawn on the back of the card 0.5 cm from the side. Cut along the line using the teeth of the scissors. Fold the cut part backwards and carefully place the teeth of the scissors in the pattern which has already been cut out. This will create a border which continues in one smooth line.

Embossing

To emboss, place the stencil on the good side of the card and secure it in place using masking tape. Place the card (with the stencil) upside down on the light box. Carefully press the paper through the opening in the stencil using an embossing pen. You only have to push around the edge to raise up the whole image.

The patterns

Full-size examples of all the patterns are given in this book. Copy them using the light box. Their large size makes the patterns easy to cut out from the card. A useful aid for copying the patterns onto the card is the transparent plastic IRIS folding and drawing template. This A4-size template has five different patterns. Specially punched cards are available for the sailboat, teapot, small butterflies, windmill, tulip, chicken, apple, heart, candle, Christmas bell, Christmas tree and double star patterns.

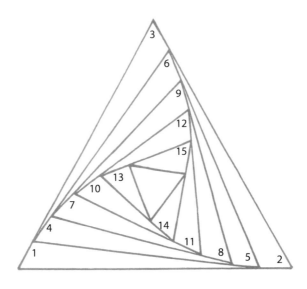

Basic triangle

Basic circle

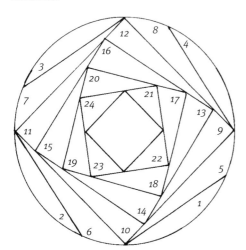

Basic square

Materials

To make the cards:

- ❏ Card: Canson Mi-Teintes (C),
  Artoz (A) and
  Papicolor (P)
- ❏ Punched cards
- ❏ Cutting knife
- ❏ Cutting mat
- ❏ Pencil
- ❏ Ruler with a metal cutting edge
- ❏ Adhesive tape
- ❏ Double-sided adhesive tape
- ❏ Masking tape
- ❏ Photo glue
- ❏ Various punches (Tom Tas, Craft Punch)
- ❏ Border ornament punches: heart, rope and spring
- ❏ Exchangeable hand punch (TomTas)
- ❏ Multi-corner punch (Reuser)
- ❏ Hand punch: flower, heart, star (Fiskars)
- ❏ Hole punch
- ❏ Scissors and silhouette scissors
- ❏ Figure scissors and corner scissors (Fiskars)
- ❏ Ridge master
- ❏ Ornare Baby decorative pricking template
  (Marianne Design)
- ❏ Circle cutter
- ❏ Gel pen
- ❏ Pink pencil
- ❏ Embossing pen
- ❏ Various embossing stencils
  (Avec, Linda Design, Make Me!)
- ❏ Bobbles

- ❏ Sticker sheets
- ❏ Light box

For the IRIS folding:

- ❏ Used envelopes from:
  - Banks
  - Insurance companies
  - Local councils
  - Companies
  - Institutions
  - Schools
  - Trade unions
  - Societies
  - Advertisements
- ❏ IRIS folding text stickers
- ❏ Green and blue IRIS folding text sheets
- ❏ Strips of Tissu paper
- ❏ Holographic paper

The middle of the card:

- ❏ Deco tape
- ❏ Holographic paper
- ❏ Shiny origami paper

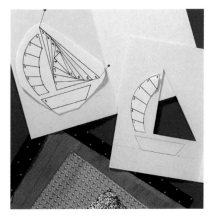

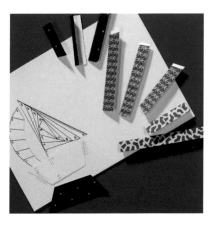

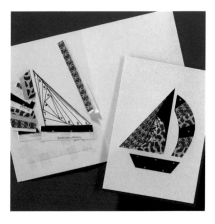

Triangle

1. Copy the pattern onto the left-hand inside of the card. Cut out the parts of the boat.

2. Cut the envelopes into strips and fold a border along their entire length. Stick the pattern to your cutting mat and place the card on top of it.

3. Place the strips from bottom to top in colours A, B and C over the spinnaker and stick down the left-hand and right-hand sides using adhesive tape.

Square

1. Copy the pattern onto the back of the card. Cut out the square.

2. Cut the envelopes into strips and fold them down. Stick the pattern to your cutting mat and place the card on top of it.

3. Place the strips exactly against the line and stick down the left-hand and right-hand sides using adhesive tape.

Circle

1. Cut the circle out of the back of the card. Cut the envelopes into strips and fold the edge over.

2. Place the pattern on your cutting mat. Place the card on top and secure the left-hand side into place. Place the strips precisely against the line and stick the left-hand and right-hand sides in place using adhesive tape.

3. Fold the card open from time to time to see whether the patterns you have made continue nicely.

4. The inside of more than three hundred envelopes.

Triangles

This basic pattern will teach you the unique method of folding and sticking used for IRIS folding.

For all the cards, follow the instructions given for the basic triangle (see Techniques, page 8).

Card 1

Card: white (14.8 x 21 cm and 14.6 x 10.3 cm) • Pattern 1A • 2 cm wide strips from 3 different blue envelopes • Butterfly punch
Punch out four butterflies. Stick two on the card using glue. Stick the bodies of the other butterflies on the butterflies already stuck on the card and fold the wings upwards. Decorate the card using an ivy embossing stencil.

Card 2

Card: dark blue (14.8 x 21 cm), grey (P20) (14.4 x 10 cm) and light lavender (P21) (14.2 x 9.7 cm) • Pattern 1A • 2 cm wide strips from 3 different pink/purple envelopes • Text sticker • Corner punch • Silver holographic paper
Cut the triangle out of the light lavender card and punch out the corners. After completing the IRIS folding, stick the cards on each other, in ascending order of size, using double-sided adhesive tape.

Card 3

Card: iris blue (P31) (14.8 x 21 cm) and white (14.8 x 10.5 cm) • Pattern 1A • 2 cm wide strips from 3 different blue envelopes • Gold holographic paper • Butterfly punch • Figure scissors • Bee stamp • Line stickers • Text sticker
Cut around the edge of the white card using the figure scissors. Stick the white card on the blue card and decorate it with butterflies, stamps, line stickers and a text sticker.

Card 4

Card: white (14.8 x 21 cm and 14.8 x 10.5 cm) • Pattern 1B • 2 cm wide strips from 3 different blue envelopes • Silver holographic paper • Figure scissors • Text sticker • Line stickers and corner stickers
Fold the card double and cut a strip off the right-hand side using figure scissors. Determine the position for the triangle and follow the instructions given for the basic triangle. Finish the card with a text sticker, corner stickers and line stickers.

Card 5

Card: grey (14.8 x 21 cm), red (14.4 x 10.1 cm) and white (14 x 9.7 cm) • Pattern 1B • 2 cm wide strips from 3 different red, purple and black-and-white envelopes • Corner punch • Origami paper
Punch out the corners of the white card.

Card 6

Card: lavender (P21) (14.8 x 21 cm), red (14.2 x 10.3 cm) and blue (13.8 x 10.3 cm) • Pattern 1B • 2 cm wide strips from 3 different red, purple and black-and-white envelopes • Figure scissors • Text sticker • Gold holographic paper

Cut around the edge of the blue card using the figure scissors.

Card 7

Card: dark blue (P41) (26.6 x 13.3 cm), lilac (12.3 x 12.3 cm) and white (12.1 x 12.1 cm) • Pattern 1A • 2 cm wide strips from 3 different purple/pink envelopes • Line stickers • Text stickers • Gold holographic paper

Punch out the corners of the white card.

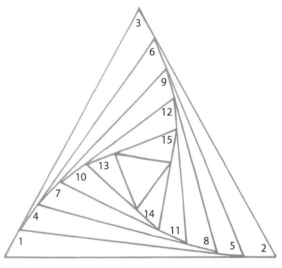

pattern 1A

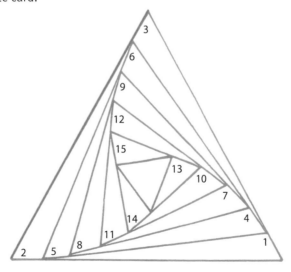

pattern 1B

Playing with triangles

Turn them to the left and right.

Or have them standing straight

up or upside down!

Card 1

*Card: blue (14.8 x 21 cm and 14.6 x 10.3 cm)
• Pattern 2A • 2 cm wide strips from three different blue/grey envelopes • Silver holographic paper*
Cut the triangles out of the left-hand side of the card. Stick the strips on the card in order, i.e. 1, 2, 3, etc. Cover the middle with holographic paper. Cut 0.4 cm wide strips from one of the envelopes and stick them on the card parallel to the triangles, as shown in the photograph.

Card 2

*Card: grey (14.8 x 21 cm) and white (14.5 x 9.6 cm)
• Pattern 2B • 2 cm wide strips from 3 different envelopes with a grey pattern • Stickers • Silver holographic paper*
Cut the diamond shape of pattern 2B out of the white card. First, make a starting strip using a strip of colour A (8 x 2 cm). Fold this strip to a size of 8 x 0.8 cm by folding over both edges. Stick the starting strip on the card according to the pattern and follow the rest of the instructions given for the basic triangle. When finished, stick it on grey card and stick line stickers on the card which go from the middle to the edge of the card. Decorate the card using a text sticker.

Card 3

Card: white (14.8 x 21 cm and 14.6 x 10.3 cm) • Pattern 2A • 2 cm wide strips from 3 different blue envelopes • Blue origami paper
Follow the instructions given for card 1. Cut 0.4 cm wide strips of colour C and stick them on the card, as shown in the photograph.

Card 4

Card: dark blue (14.8 x 21 cm and 14.8 x 9.5 cm) • Pattern 2C • 2 cm wide strips from 3 different blue envelopes • Silver holographic paper
Cut the diamond shape out of the smallest card. Start with the starting strip, as explained for pattern 2B, and follow the rest of the instructions given for the basic triangle. To finish the card,

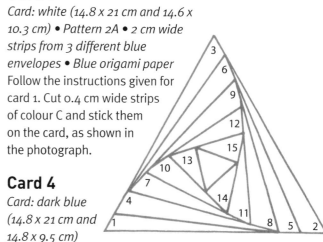

pattern 2A

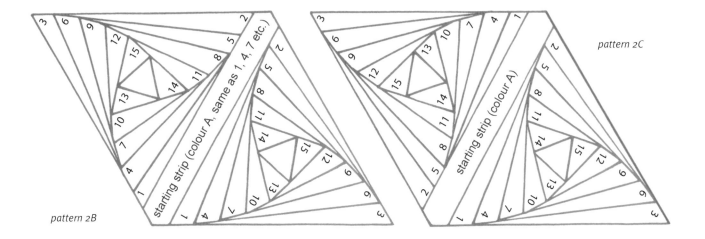

pattern 2B

pattern 2C

cut two strips of colour A (14.8 x 1 cm) and stick them on the back of the card on the left-hand and right-hand sides so that 1 mm is visible on the front of the card. Stick all of this on the double card.

Card 5

Card: dark blue (14.8 x 21 cm) and white (13.8 x 10 cm) • Sheet of envelope paper (colour A) (14.6 x 10.3 cm) • Pattern 2B • 2 cm wide strips from 3 different grey/blue envelopes • Corner punch • Text sticker • Silver holographic paper
Cut the diamond shape out of the white card and punch out the corners. Make a starting strip of colour A as described for card 2 and follow the instructions given for the basic triangle. Stick the white card on the sheet of envelope paper and stick this on the dark blue card. Decorate the card using a text sticker.

Card 6

Card: white (14.8 x 21 cm and 14.6 x 10.3 cm) • Pattern 2B • 2 cm wide strips from 3 different blue

envelopes • Stickers • Corner scissors • Silver holographic paper
Start with a starting strip of colour A. Follow the instructions given for card 1. Stick the covering card against the back of the pattern to cover it over.
Cut off two corners of the top card using the corner scissors and stick two corner stickers on the bottom card. Decorate the card using border stickers and a text sticker.

Card 7

Card: red (14.8 x 21 cm) and white (14.6 x 9.6 cm) • Pattern 2B • 2 cm wide strips from 2 different grey envelopes and a red envelope • Stickers • Corner punch • Silver holographic paper
Punch out the corners of the white card. The starting strip of colour A is the start of two IRIS folding triangles. Stick the finished IRIS folding card on the red card. Finish the card with line stickers and a text sticker.

Boats

A suitable card for a
wedding, a long holiday
or a new job.

*All the cards are made according
to the instructions given for card 1.*

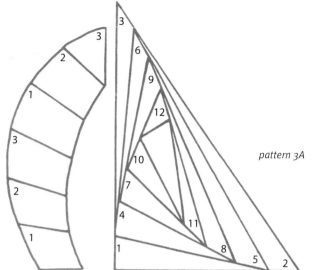

pattern 3A

Card 1

*Card: white (14.8 x 21 cm and 14.6 x 10.3 cm)
• Pattern 3A • 2 cm and 3 cm wide strips from
three different blue envelopes • Stickers • Silver
holographic paper*
Cut out the boat as described in Techniques. Cover
the hull with a 2 cm wide strip of colour C which has
not been folded. Fold the 3 cm wide strips down and
use them to cover the spinnaker. Follow the instructions given for the basic triangle. Decorate the card
using line stickers and a text sticker.

Card 2

*Card: silver grey (P02) (14.8 x 21 cm) and dark
blue (P41) (14.8 x 10.5 cm) • Pattern 3B •
2 cm and 3 cm wide strips from dark blue, white
and blue, and sea green and white envelopes •
Silver holographic paper • Text sticker • Figure
scissors*
Cut around the edge of the dark blue card using the

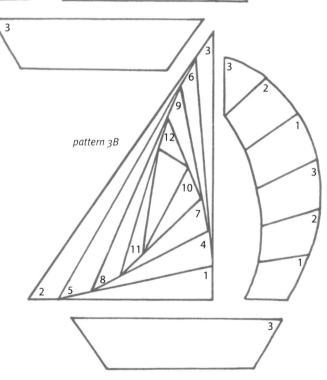

pattern 3B

figure scissors. Stick the darker card on the double card and stick a text sticker on it.

Card 3

Card: blue (P06) (14.8 x 21 cm) and white (14.8 x 10.5 cm) • Pattern 3A • 2 cm and 3 cm wide strips from three different blue envelopes • Blue/green origami paper • Figure scissors
Cut around the edge of the white card using the figure scissors. Stick the white card on the blue card.

Card 4

Card: white (14.8 x 21 cm and 14.6 x 10.3 cm) • Pattern 3A • 2 cm and 3 cm wide strips from 3 different blue envelopes • Silver holographic paper • Ridge master • Gel pen • Sticker

For this card, the boat sails along the longer side of the card. Run the bottom corners through the ridge master. Decorate the card using the gel pens. Stick the covering card against the inside of the card.

Card 5

Card: blue (P6) (14.8 x 21 cm and 14.6 x 10.3 cm) • Pattern 3A • 2 cm and 3 cm wide strips from 3 different blue envelopes • Silver holographic paper
Cover the hull (colour C) and the spinnaker (colour A) with a piece of envelope paper which has not been folded. Cut out waves and birds in colour C and stick them on the card.

Balloons and kites

Go flying!

The balloons are made according to the instructions given for card 1. The kites are made according to the instructions given for card 2.

Card 1

Card: green (14.8 x 21 cm) and white (13.7 x 9.6 cm) • Sheet of envelope paper (14.3 x 10 cm) • Pattern 4A • 2 cm wide strips from 4 different green envelopes • Two 4 cm wide strips of colour A for sections 1 and 5 • Silver holographic paper • Black fine-liner • Text sticker

Punch out the corners of the white card using a corner punch. Draw the outer lines of the balloon and the basket on the white card and cut out both shapes (note: not the ropes!). Cover the basket with a piece of unfolded envelope paper in the colour of your choice. Follow the instructions given for the basic triangle. Draw the ropes with a fine-liner and draw speed lines. Stick the white card on the sheet of envelope paper and then stick everything on the green card.

Card 2

Card: light blue (P19) (14.8 x 21 cm) and blue (P31) (14 x 9.8 cm) • Pattern 4B • Butterfly corner punch • 3 cm wide strips from 4 different blue and dark blue envelopes • Silver holographic paper

Punch butterflies in the corners of the blue card. Cut out the kite and fill it with the strips of envelope paper. Make a tail for the kite using bows and a piece of string.

Card 3

Card: blue (P42) (14.8 x 21 cm and 14.6 x 10.3 cm) • Pattern 4A • 2 cm wide strips from 4 different blue envelopes • Two 4 cm wide strips of colour A for sections 1 and 5 • Silver holographic paper

Card 4

Card: green (P18) (14.8 x 21 cm) and rainbow green (14.4 x 10.2 cm) • Sheet of envelope paper (14.4 x 10.2 cm) in colour D • Pattern 4B • 4 cm wide strips from 4 different green envelopes • Silver holographic paper • Figure scissors • Green thread

Cut around the edge of the rainbow card using the figure scissors. Decorate the card with some thread. Stick the card on

pattern 4A

the sheet of envelope paper and then stick everything on the green card.

Card 5

Card: cherry-red (P33) (14.8 x 21 cm) and rainbow pink (13.8 x 9.4 cm) • Pattern 4B • Heart corner punch • 4 cm wide strips from 4 different beige/pink envelopes • Gold holographic paper
Punch out the corners.

Card 6

Card: brown (P39) (14.8 x 21 cm) and cream (14.2 x 10.2 cm) • Pattern 4A • 2 cm wide strips from 4 different red/bruin envelopes • Two 4 cm wide strips of colour A • Gold holographic paper • Corner punch
Punch out the corners.

Card 7

Card: light brown (14.8 x 21 cm) and yellow (P29) (14 x 10 cm) • Sheet of orange envelope paper (14 x 10 cm) • Pattern 4A • 2 cm wide strips from different brown/orange/yellow envelopes • Two 4 cm wide strips of colour A • Gold holographic paper • Figure scissors • Sticker
Cut around the edge of the yellow card using the figure scissors.

Card 8

Card: red (P43) (14.8 x 21 cm) and cream (13.8 x 9.6 cm) • Pattern 4A • 2 cm wide strips from 4

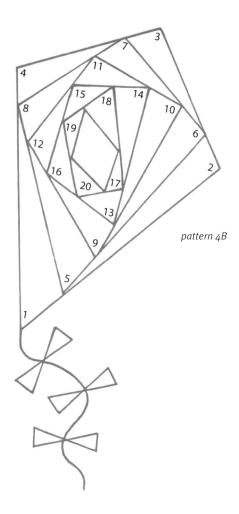

pattern 4B

different red/pink envelopes • Two 4 cm wide strips of colour A • Gold-and-red holographic paper • Heart corner punch
Punch out the corners.

Tea pots

For this model, you will not need 3 or 4, but 5 different envelopes which match and contrast each other nicely.

All the cards are made according to the instructions given for card 1.

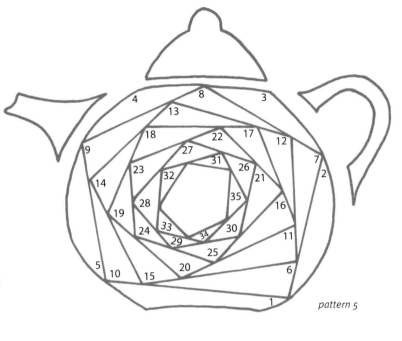

pattern 5

Card 1
Card: carnation white (P03) (13.3 x 26.6 cm) and brown (P39) (12 x 12 cm) • Pattern 5 • 2 cm wide strips from 5 different beige envelopes • Gold holographic paper • Cloud corner punch
Punch out the corners of the brown card. Cut out the pot (not the lid, the spout or the handle). Fill the pot with the strips as described for the basic triangle. Cut out the lid, the spout and the handle from envelope paper (colour B) and stick them around the pot on the front of the card.

Card 2
Card: green (P18) (13.3 x 26.6 cm) and white (P30) (12.4 x 12.4 cm) • Pattern 5 • 2 cm wide strips from

5 different green envelopes • Silver holographic paper • Lily corner punch
Punch out the corners of the white card.

Card 3

Card: cloudy blue-grey (P52) (13.3 x 26.6 cm) and dark blue (P41) (12.6 x 12.6 cm) • Pattern 5 • 2 cm wide strips from 5 different grey envelopes • Silver holographic paper

Card 4

Card: brown (P39) (13.3 x 26.6 cm) and yellow (P29) (12 x 12 cm) • Pattern 5 • 2 cm wide strips from 5 different beige/brown/red envelopes •

Silver holographic paper • Heart corner punch
Punch out the corners of the yellow card.

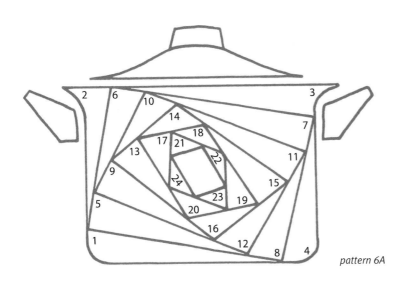

pattern 6A

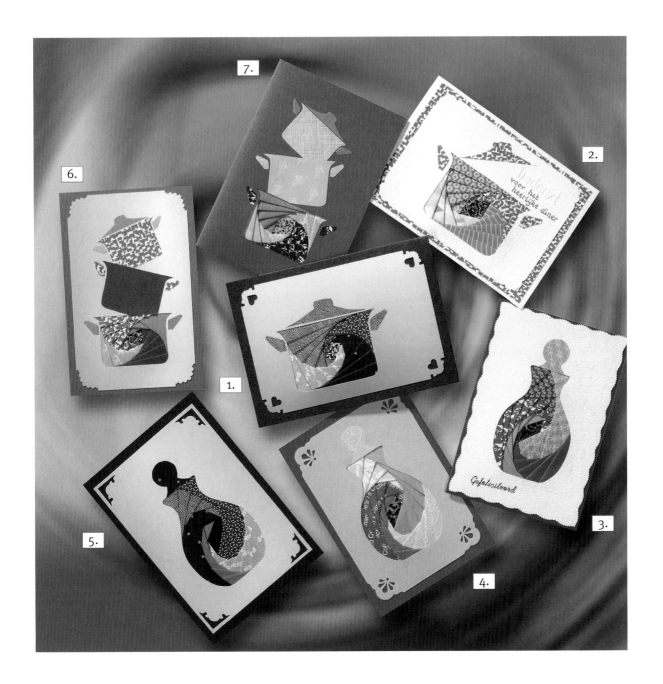

Pots and pans

An invitation to or a thank you for a dinner or an enjoyable evening.

Card 1

Card: dark blue (14.8 x 21 cm) and rainbow blue (14 x 9.6 cm) • Pattern 6A (page 29) • 2.5 cm strips from 4 different blue envelopes • Silver holographic paper • Heart corner punch

Cut out the pan (not the lid or the handles) from the rainbow card. Fill the hole with the strips of envelope paper. Turn the card over. Cut out the lid and the handles from envelope paper (colour C) and stick them on the card.

Card 2

Card: white (14.8 x 21 cm and 12.8 x 9.4 cm) • Sheet of envelope paper in colour B (14 x 9.8 cm) • Pattern 6A (page 29) • 2.5 cm wide strips from 4 different envelopes • Gold holographic paper • Corner punch • Linda Design embossing stencil

Cut the pan out of a landscape-shape card. Follow the instructions given for card 1.

Card 3

Card: brick red (P35) (14.8 x 21 cm) and white (14.8 x 10.5 cm) • Pattern 6B • 3 cm wide strips from 5 different brown/green envelopes • Gold

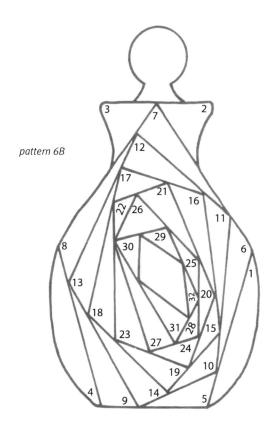

pattern 6B

holographic paper • Figure scissors • Text sticker

Cut around the edge of the white card using the figure scissors. Cut out the bottle (not the top) and fill it with strips of envelope paper. Cut out the top from envelope paper (colour C) and stick it above the bottle. Stick everything on the red card. Pay attention: colour B stops after section 22!

Card 4

Card: cherry-red (P33) (14.8 x 21 cm) and light grey (13.4 x 9.4 cm) • Pattern 6B • 3 cm wide strips from 5 different pink/red envelopes • Gold holographic paper • Corner punch

Punch out the corners of the light grey card and follow the instructions given for card 3.

Card 5

Card: dark blue (14.8 x 21 cm) and rainbow blue (14 x 9.8 cm) • Pattern 6B • 3 cm strips from 5 different blue envelopes • Blue origami paper • Lily corner punch

Punch out the corners and follow the instructions given for card 3.

Card 6

Card: green (P16) (14.8 x 21 cm) and rainbow beige (14.3 x 9 cm) • Pattern 6C • 2 cm wide strips from 4 different green and beige envelopes • Gold holographic paper • Cloud corner punch

Punch out the corners of the beige card. Cut out the bottom pan (not the handles) and fill it with the strips of envelope paper. Cut the other pans, the handles and the lid out of scrap pieces of envelope paper and stick them on the card according to the pattern.

Card 7

Card: cherry-red (P33) (14.8 x 21 cm and 14.4 x 10.1 cm) • Pattern 6C • 2 cm wide strips

from 4 different grey envelopes • Silver holographic paper

Follow the instructions given for card 6.

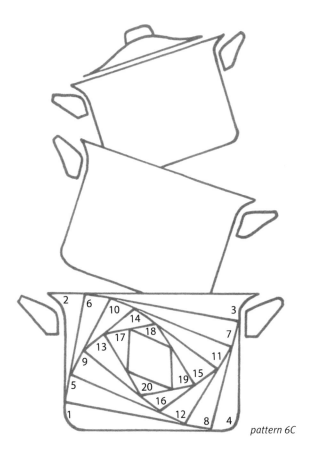

pattern 6C

Windmills

The triangle, boat and windmill cards are all predominantly men's cards.

All the cards are made according to the instructions given for card 1.

Card 1

Card: iris blue (P31) (13.3 x 26.6 cm) and carnation white (P03) (12.2 x 12.2 cm) • Pattern 7 • 2 cm wide strips from 3 different blue envelopes • Silver holographic paper

Carefully cut out the pattern's four large triangles. Fill the holes according to the instructions given for the basic triangle.

Cut the four small triangles out of envelope paper (colour B) and stick them on the card according to the pattern. Stick everything on the blue card.

Card 2

Card: iris blue (P31) (13.3 x 26.6 cm) and lilac (P37) (12.5 x 12.5 cm) • Pattern 7 • 2 cm wide strips from 3 different blue envelopes • Silver holographic paper

Card 3

Card: dark blue (P 41) (13.3 x 26.6 cm), light lavender (P 20) (12.6 x 12.6 cm), iris blue (P31) (12.4 x 12.4 cm) and light yellow (P29) (12.4 x 12.4 cm) • Pattern 7 • 2 cm wide strips from 3 different blue envelopes • Figure scissors • Silver holographic paper

Cut around the edge of the light yellow card using the figure scissors.

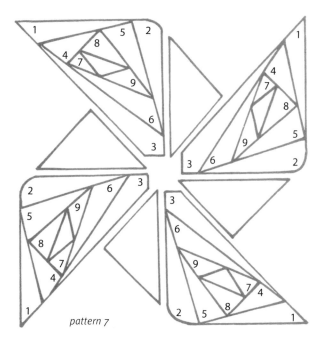

pattern 7

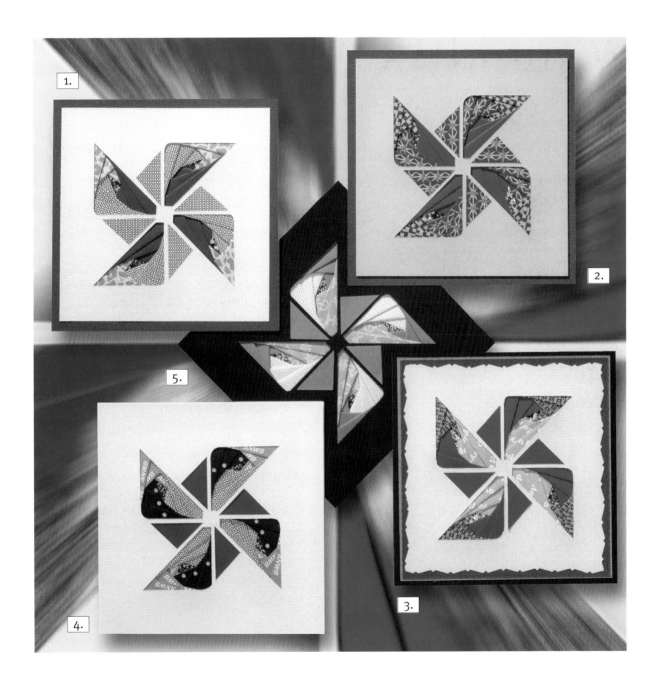

Card 4

Card: white (13.3 x 26.6 cm and 13 x 13.3 cm)
• Pattern 7 • 2 cm wide strips from 3 different
blue envelopes • Red holographic paper

Card 5

Card: dark blue (13.3 x 26.6 cm and 13 x 13.3 cm)
• Pattern 7 • 2 cm wide strips from 3 different
blue/white envelopes • Silver holographic paper

Fluttering butterflies

Attractive cards which are

suitable for using brightly

coloured envelopes.

*Cards 1 to 3 are made according to the
instructions given for card 1. Cards 4 to 7
are made according to the instructions
given for card 4.*

Card 1

*Card: dark blue (P41) (13.3 x 26.6 cm) and white
(11.8 x 11.8 cm) • Pattern 8A • 2 cm wide strips
from 4 different blue envelopes • Butterfly corner
punch • Silver holographic paper*
Cut both wings out of the white card. Punch out the
corners. Follow the instructions given for the basic
triangle. Cut the body and the antennas out of a
scrap piece of envelope paper and stick them on
the card.

Card 2

*Card: carnation white (P03) (13.3 x 26.6 cm) and
blue (P06) (13.3 x 13.3 cm) • Pattern 8A • 2 cm
wide strips from 4 different blue envelopes • Blue
holographic paper*
Cut slanting corners on the front site of the
carnation white card as shown in the pattern

on page 37. Once the wings have been filled, stick
small pieces of double-sided adhesive tape on the
inside of the white card on the left-hand side.
Place the blue card exactly along the edge of the
white card.

Card 3

*Card: white (13.3 x 26.6 cm and 12.7 x 12.7 cm)
and dark blue (12.7 x 12.7 cm) • Pattern 8A •
2 cm wide strips from 4 different blue envelopes
• Silver holographic paper • Stickers*
Cut slanting corners on the small white card.

Card 4

*Card: iris blue (P31) (14.8 x 21 cm) and rainbow
pink (14.6 x 9.5 cm) • Pattern 8B • 1.5 cm wide
strips from 4 different pink, red, purple and
blue envelopes • Heart corner punch • Fine-liner
• Origami paper*
Cut the four wings out of the rainbow card. Punch

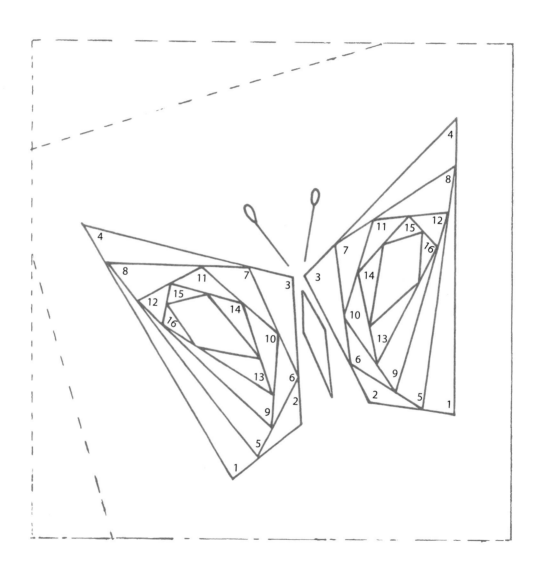

pattern 8A

out the corners and fill the wings. Cut the bodies out of a scrap piece of blue paper and draw the antennas.

Card 5

Card: sky blue (P04) (14.8 x 21 cm) and Christmas green(P18) (14.2 x 10.2 cm) • Pattern 8B • 1.5 cm wide strips from 4 different yellow/green envelopes • Gold holographic paper
Cut slanting corners on the dark green card as shown in the photograph and fill the wings with strips of envelope paper. Give the butterflies a yellow body and antennas.

Card 6

Card: cherry-red (P33) (14.8 x 21 cm) and rainbow orange (14.6 x 10.3 cm) • Pattern 8B • 1.5 cm wide strips from 4 different orange/red envelopes • Gold holographic paper • Lily corner punch
Punch out the corners.

Card 7

Card: green (P16) (14.8 x 21 cm and 14.4 x 10.1 cm) • Pattern 8B • 1.5 cm wide strips from 4 different beige/brown/light green envelopes • Silver holographic paper

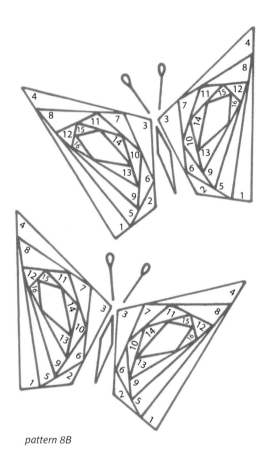

pattern 8B

Circles

Circles in different colours

flavours!

For all cards, follow the instructions for the basic circle (see Techniques)

Card 1

Card: cornflower blue A425 (14.8 x 21 cm) and lilac C104 (13.2 x 9.3 cm) • Pattern 1 • 2 cm wide strips from 4 different blue envelopes • Silver holographic paper • Circle cutter
Cut a Ø 6 cm circle in the middle of the lilac paper

Card 2

Card: honey yellow A243 (13 x 26 cm and 10 x 10 cm) • Pattern 1 • 2 cm wide strips from 4 different beige and brown envelopes • Gold deco tape • Circle cutter
Cut a Ø 6 cm circle out from the inside of the left-hand half of the card. After finishing the IRIS folding, cover the design with the small card. Cutting tip for decorating: cut 1 mm strips of envelope paper. They will curl up themselves into a nice curve.

Card 3

Card: violet C507 (14.8 x 21 cm) and lilac C104 (12.8 x 9 cm) • Pattern 1 • 2 cm wide strips from 4 different purple envelopes, such as from advertising, an internet provider and a university • Silver holographic paper • Circle cutter

Card 4

Card: lilac C104 (14.8 x 21 cm) and violet C507 (13 x 9 cm) • Pattern 1 • 2 cm wide strips from 4 different purple envelopes from a university, hospital, wine guild and insurance company • Silver holographic paper • Circle cutter

Card 5

Card: aquamarine A363 (13 x 26 cm and 10 x 10 cm) • Pattern 1 • 2 cm wide strips from 4 different aquamarine envelopes • 11 x 11 cm envelope paper (colour A) • Silver deco tape • Circle cutter

After the IRIS folding, decorate the front of the card with circles of envelope paper. Cutting tip: first, cut the circles out to Ø 10 cm and then cut them to Ø 9.6 cm. Cut the small circle to Ø 8 cm and then to Ø 7.6 cm. Place them around the circle you have just made and stick them in place using a small amount of glue.

Card 6

Card: azure C590 (14.8 x 21 cm) and soft blue C102 (14 x 9.5 cm) • Pattern 1 • 2 cm wide strips from 4 different blue and green envelopes • Silver deco tape • Circle cutter

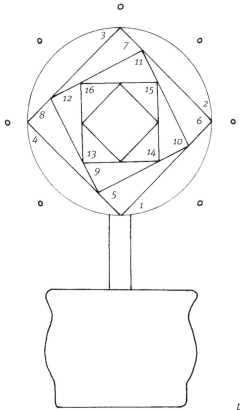

pattern 2

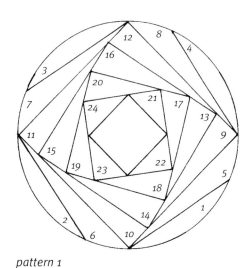

pattern 1

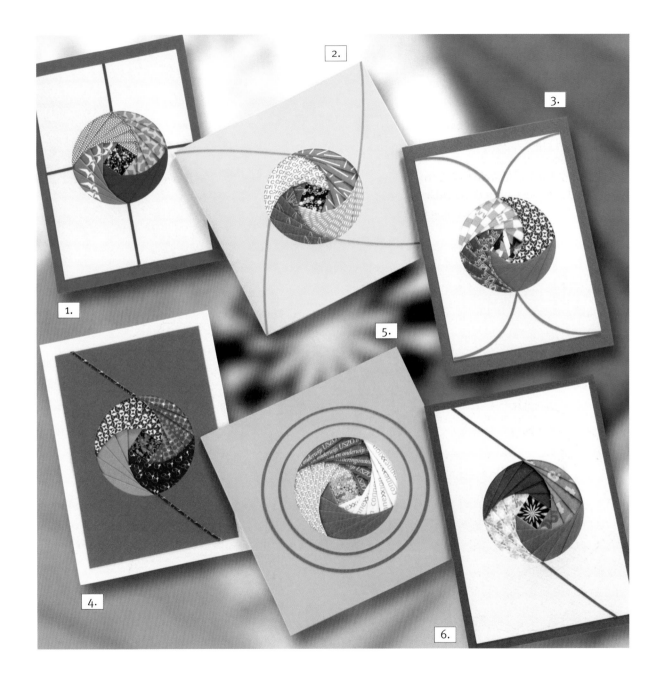

Playing with circles

These round trees love

the sun.

The sun is made according to the description for card 1.

Card 1

Card: honey yellow A243 (14.8 x 21 cm) and lobster red A545 (14 x 9.8 cm) • Pattern 2 (page 42) • 2 cm wide strips from 4 different brown and orange envelopes • 10 x 10 cm envelope paper (colour B). Gold holographic paper • Circle cutter • Cloud corner punch

Cut a Ø 5 cm circle out of the middle of the red card and punch out the corners. Turn pattern 2 45 degrees anticlockwise, so that section 1 is horizontal. Follow the instructions given for the basic circle. Cutting tip: copy half of the sun ray border on the right-hand side of the back of the envelope paper. Fold it in two and stick it together with staples. Cut out the sun rays first and then the semicircle. Stick the sun on the card.

Card 2

Card: honey yellow A243 (14.8 x 21 cm), dark blue A417 (14 x 10 cm) and light yellow A241 (13.7 x 9.5 cm) • Pattern 2 (page 42) • 2 cm wide strips from 4 different yellow and beige envelopes

• 10 x 10 cm envelope paper (colour A) • Gold holographic paper • Circle cutter • Victorian embossing stencil
Emboss the smallest card.

Card 3

Card: blue and orange duo-colour card (14.8 x 21 cm) and a covering circle (Ø 9 cm) of the same material • Pattern 2 (page 42) • 2 cm wide strips from 4 different yellow envelopes • 10 x 10 cm orange envelope paper • Copper red deco tape • Circle cutter • Regal corner scissors • Sun mini punch

Cut the Ø 5 cm circle out of the left-hand inner card. Cut two corners using the corner scissors. Punch out orange suns.

Card 4

Card: butter yellow C400 (14.8 x 21 cm) and royal blue A427 (11.7 x 9.7 cm) • Pattern 2 (page 42) • 2 cm wide strips from 4 different orange and yellow envelopes • 10 x 10 cm envelope paper (colour C) • Gold deco tape • Circle cutter • Sun embossing stencil • Regal corner scissors

Cut the corners of the blue card and cut out the circle. Emboss the corners of the yellow card.

Card 5

Card: off-white C335 (14.8 x 21 cm) and dark green C448 (14.4 x 10 cm) • Pattern 2 (page 42) • 2 cm wide strips from 4 different red and green envelopes

• *Gold holographic paper* • *Flower hand punch*
• *Bow punch*
Cut a Ø 5 cm circle out of the left-hand inner card approximately 5.5 cm from the top. Punch out flowers along the edge of the circle. Cover these with pieces of envelope paper and finish it off as described for a basic circle. Cover the worked area with the small card. Copy the flower pot and the stem onto the back of the envelope paper. Cut them out and stick them on the card together with the bow and the flowers.

Halo

Card 6

Card: resin brown C336 (14.8 x 21 cm) and dark pink C350 (13.7 x 9.5 cm) • *Pattern 2 (page 42)* • *2 cm wide strips from 4 different pink and beige envelopes* • *Gold deco tape* • *Round flower frame embossing stencil* • *Pink pencil*
Cut the Ø 5 cm circle out of the pink card and emboss the border. Colour in the flowers.

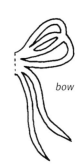

bow

Card 7

Card: cerise P33 (14.8 x 21 cm) and carnation white P03 (14.2 x 8.8 cm) • *14.5 x 9.3 cm purple envelope paper* • *Pattern 2 (page 42)* • *2 cm wide strips from 4 different purple, lilac, red and beige envelopes* • *Silver deco tape* • *Victorian embossing stencil* • *Flower corner punch* • *Bow punch* • *Dove hand punch*
Cut the Ø 5 cm circle out of the white card. Emboss the border and punch out two corners. Punch out the doves and the bow.

Card 8

Card: lemon yellow C101 (14.8 x 21 cm) and almond green C480 (14.6 x 10.3 cm) • *Pattern 2 (page 42)* • *2 cm wide strips from 4 different green envelopes* • *Silver deco tape* • *Flower hand punch*
Rotate pattern 2 45 degrees anticlockwise so that section 1 is horizontal.

Tulips

Spring is in the air.

All the cards are made according to the description given for card 1.

Card on page 2

Card: bright red C506 (14.8 x 21 cm), light orange C553 (14.4 x 9.3 cm) and white (14 x 8.6 cm)
• Pattern 5 • 2 cm wide strips from 5 different orange and red envelopes • 6 x 6 cm green envelope paper • Silver deco tape

Card 1

Card: dark blue (14.8 x 21 cm), lilac C507 (14.2 x 9.7 cm) and ivory C111 (14 x 9.5 cm) • Pattern 4 • 2 cm wide strips from 5 different green, pink-red and purple envelopes • 6 x 6 cm envelope paper (colour A) • Gold holographic paper • Multi-corner punch • Text embossing stencil

Punch out the corners, emboss the text and cut the flower out of the ivory card. Finish it off as described for a basic circle. Copy the stem and the leaves onto the back of the envelope paper (colour A) using the light box. Cut these out and stick them onto the front.

Card 2

Card: shell-white C112 (14.8 x 21 cm), beige C374 (13.5 x 9.4 cm) and indigo blue C140 (13 x 8.7 cm)

• Pattern 4 • 2 cm wide strips from 5 different beige envelopes • 6 x 6 cm envelope paper (colour A)
• Gold holographic paper • Butterfly corner punch
Punch out the top corners of the blue card.

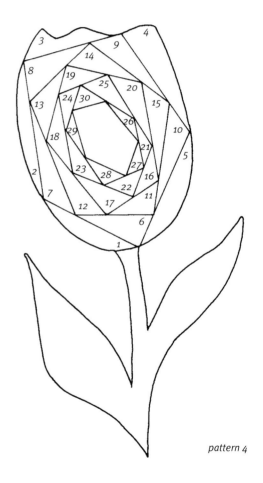

pattern 4

Card 3

Card: dark green C448 (14.8 x 21 cm), butter yellow C400 (13.4 x 9.2 cm) and off-white C335 (13 x 8.8 cm) • Pattern 5 • 2 cm wide strips from 5 different yellow and green envelopes • 6 x 6 cm envelope paper (colour A) • Gold deco tape • Tulip punch
Punch the tulips out of the white card.

Card 4

Card: dark green C448 (14.8 x 21 cm) and lily-white C110 (14.2 x 9.5 cm) • Pattern 4 • 2 cm wide strips from 5 different purple, pink and green envelopes from Foster Parents, a wine guild and an insurance company • 6 x 6 cm envelope paper (colour A)
• Flamed deco tape • Ornamental corner punch
• Tulip punch
Punch out the corners of the white card.
Punch the small tulips out of the envelope paper (colour A).

Labels (patterns 3, 10 and 14)

Almost all the labels are made out of a 7 x 11 cm card and a cover card measuring 6.8 x 5.2 cm. The shape of both the flag and the heart are cut out of the inner left-hand side of the card, which is then filled with left-over strips of envelope paper. The tulips are cut out of a 6.4 x 4.8 cm card and, after IRIS folding, this card is stuck on the card which measures 7 x 11 cm. The final size of the gift labels is 7 x 5.5 cm.

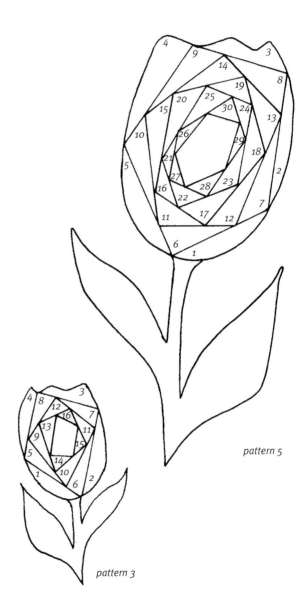

pattern 5

pattern 3

Chickens

Spring: a time for new life!

All the cards are made according to the description given for card 1.

Card 1

Card: butter yellow C400 (13.3 x 26.6 cm), salmon beige C384 (11.4 x 11.4 cm) and lily-white C110 (11.1 x 11.1 cm) • Pattern 6 • 2 cm wide strips from 4 different orange, beige and yellow envelopes • 3 x 3 cm envelope paper (colour D) • Gold deco tape • Hole punch • Mini shell figure scissors • Spring embossing stencil

Emboss two birds and cut the chicken shape out of the back of the white card (not the beak or the feet). For section 4a, use the figure scissors to cut a border along one side of the envelope paper which measures 3 x 3 cm; this piece will not be folded. Fill the chicken with strips according to the instructions for a basic circle. Note that colour A stops at section 17, therefore, section 21 is not included. Cut the beak and the feet out of the envelope paper (colour C). Make the eye from deco tape using the hole punch.

Card 2

Card: dark pink C350 (13.3 x 26.6 cm), golden yellow C374 (11 x 11 cm) and indigo blue C140 (10.3 x 10.3 cm) • Pattern 6 • 2 cm wide strips from 4 different soft orange and yellow envelopes • 3 x 3 cm envelope paper (colour D) • Gold deco tape • Hole punch • Shell figure scissors • Flower corner punch

Punch out the corners and cut out the chicken from the blue card.

Card 3

Card: sienna C374 (13 x 26 cm), bright red C506 (11.5 x 11.5 cm) and off-white (11 x 11 cm) • Pattern 6 • 2 cm wide strips from 4 different yellow envelopes • 3 x 3 cm envelope paper (colour D) • Gold holographic paper • Hole punch • Shell figure scissors • Multi-corner punch

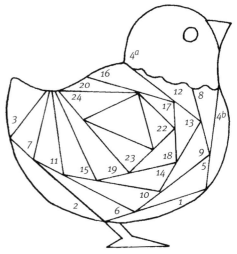

pattern 6

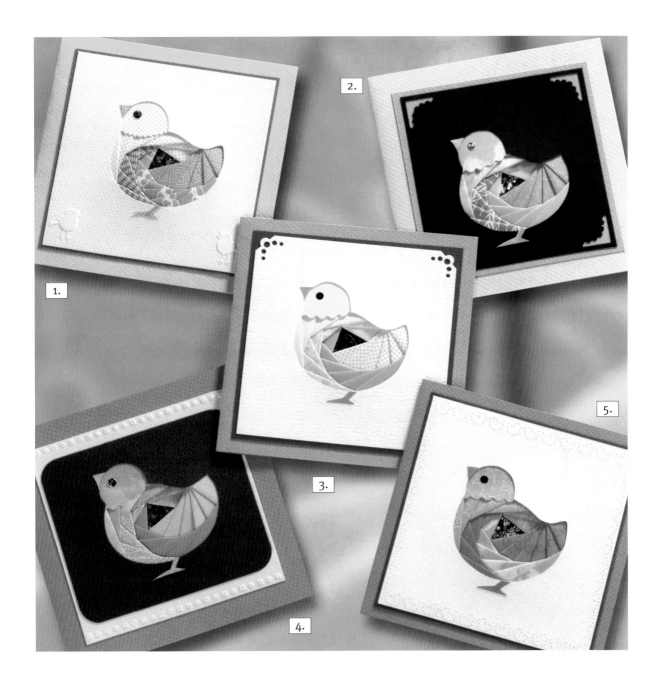

Punch out the top corners and cut out the chicken from the white card.

Card 4

Card: almond green C480 (13.3 x 26.6 cm), ivory C111 (10.8 x 10.8 cm) and dark green C448 (9 x 10.5 cm) • Pattern 6 • 2 cm wide strips from 4 different beige, yellow and soft green envelopes • 3 x 3 cm envelope paper (colour D) • Gold deco tape • Hole punch • Shell figure scissors • Regal corner punch • Geometric embossing stencil
Cut out the corners and cut out the chicken from the dark green card. Emboss the top and bottom border of the white card.

Card 5

Card: light orange C553 (13 x 26 cm), lavender blue C150 (11.8 x 11.8 cm) and off-white (11.4 x 11.4 cm) • Pattern 6 • 2 cm wide strips from 4 different orange envelopes • 3 x 3 cm envelope paper (colour D) • Gold deco tape • Hole punch • Shell figure scissors • Baby decorative pricking stencil
Place the decorative pricking stencil on the back

of the white card. Prick the chickens along the top and bottom and prick a decorative border along the sides.

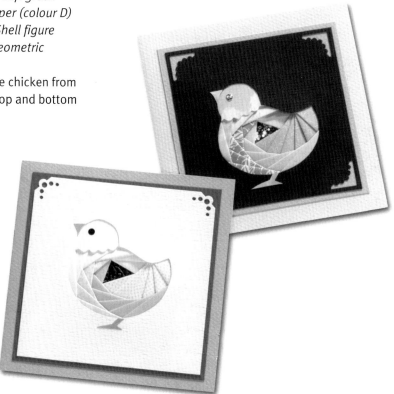

Apples

Nice juicy apples!

All the cards are made according to the instructions given for card 1.
Four different envelopes are used in each apple.

Cut the apple from the white card (not the stem or the leaves). Do the IRIS folding as described for the basic circle. Copy the stem, the leaves and the calyx onto the back of green envelope paper. Cutting tip: turn the paper using the hand which holds the paper. Stick the cut out pieces above and below the apple.

Card 2
Card: dark green C448 (13.3 x 26.6 cm), resin brown C336 (10.5 x 10.5 cm) and off-white C335 (10 x 10 cm) • Pattern 7 • 2 cm wide strips from different beige, light orange, red and grey-green envelopes • Gold holographic paper • Ornamental embossing stencil
Emboss the corners of the smallest card.

Card 1 (also shown on page 2)
Card: apple green C475 (13 x 26 cm), dark green C448 (10.5 x 10.5 cm) and off-white C335 (10 x 10 cm) • Pattern 7 • 2 cm wide strips from 4 different green envelopes • Gold deco tape

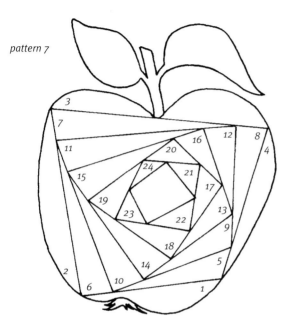

pattern 7

• *Pattern 7* • *2 cm wide strips from different green, grey and light yellow envelopes* • *Silver deco tape* • *Regal corner scissors*

Cut the corners of the almond green card with the corner scissors. Round off the corners of the white card using the corner scissors and cut out the apple.

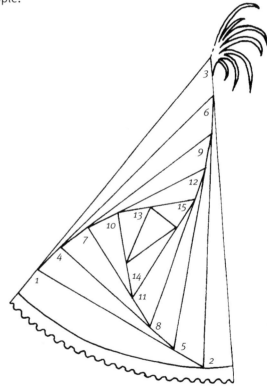

Card 3

Card: green (13 x 26 cm) and off-white C335 (11 x 11 cm) • *Pattern 7* • *2 cm wide strips from different beige, light orange, red and grey-green envelopes from, for example, a publisher, insurance company and wine guild* • *Silver deco tape* • *Multi-corner punch*

Punch out the corners of the white card and cut out the apple.

Card 4

Card: dark green C448 (13 x 26 cm), almond green C480 (12 x 12 cm) and off-white C335 (11 x 11 cm)

pattern 8

Party!

A party hat, flags and a balloon.

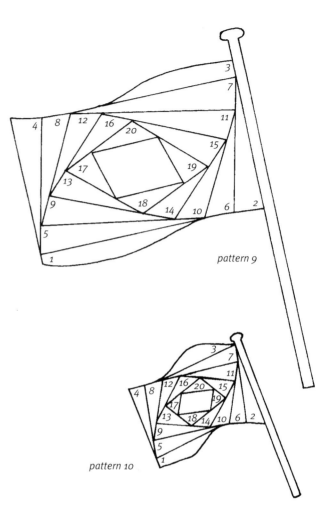

pattern 9

pattern 10

Card 1

*Card: white (14.8 x 21 cm), orange (13.9 x 9.7 cm)
and red (13.4 x 9.2 cm) • Pattern 9 • 2 cm wide
strips from 4 different blue and red envelopes
• Silver holographic paper • Multi-corner punch*
Punch out the right-hand corners and cut out the
flag from the back of the red card. Fill the flag with
strips. Cut the flagpole out of blue envelope paper
and stick it on the card.

Card 2

*Card: azure P04 (14.8 x 21 cm) and white (13.8 x
9.5 cm) • Pattern 11 • 2 cm wide strips of 4
aquamarine envelopes • Silver holographic paper
• Balloon punch • Embroidery silk*
Cut the balloon from the white paper.

Card 3

*Card: azure C590 (14.8 x 21 cm) and white
(13 x 9.5 cm) • Pattern 8 (page 54) • 2 cm wide
strips from 3 different blue envelopes • Silver
holographic paper • Multi-corner punch • Mini
shell figure scissors*
Punch out the corners of the white card and cut
out the hat. Decorate the bottom with a border
of envelope paper. Cutting tip: fold 2 x 4 cm of
envelope paper double so that it measures 2 x 2 cm
and cut the half feather along the line of the fold.

Card 4

*Card: carnation white P03 (14.8 x 21 cm) and
turquoise C595 (13.5 x 9 cm) • Pattern 11 •
2 cm wide strips from 4 different green and yellow
envelopes • Silver holographic paper • Multi-corner
punch • Embroidery silk*
Punch out the corners of the smallest card.

Card 5

Card: azure Po4 (14.8 x 21 cm) and off-white (12.8 x 9.6 cm) • 13.2 x 10 cm envelope paper (colour D) • Pattern 9 • 2 cm wide strips from 4 different blue envelopes • Silver holographic paper • Multi-corner punch
Punch out the right-hand corners.

Card 6

Card: white (14.8 x 21 cm) and blue (14.6 x 10.3 cm) • Pattern 9 • 2 cm wide strips from 4 different red, white and blue envelopes • Silver holographic paper • Scrap pieces of red and blue card
Cut the flag out of the left-hand inner card. After the IRIS folding, cover with the blue card. Decorate with the scrap pieces of card.

Card 7

Card: red C505 (14.8 x 21 cm) and white (13.8 x 9.5 cm) • Pattern 11 • 2 cm wide strips from 4 different red envelopes • Silver holographic paper • Butterfly embossing stencil • Butterfly punch • Regal corner scissors • Embroidery silk
Cut round corners and cut the balloon out of the white card. Emboss the butterflies. Stick the punched out butterflies on the embossed butterflies.

Card 8

Card: carnation white Po3 (14.8 x 21 cm) and iris blue P31 (13.2 x 9 cm) • Pattern 8 (page 54) •
2 cm wide strips of 3 purple and white envelopes • Silver deco tape • Mini shell figure scissors • Diamond corner punch
Punch out the corners and cut the hat from the blue card.

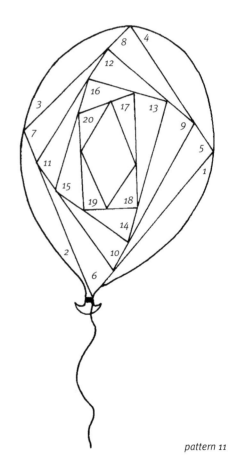

pattern 11

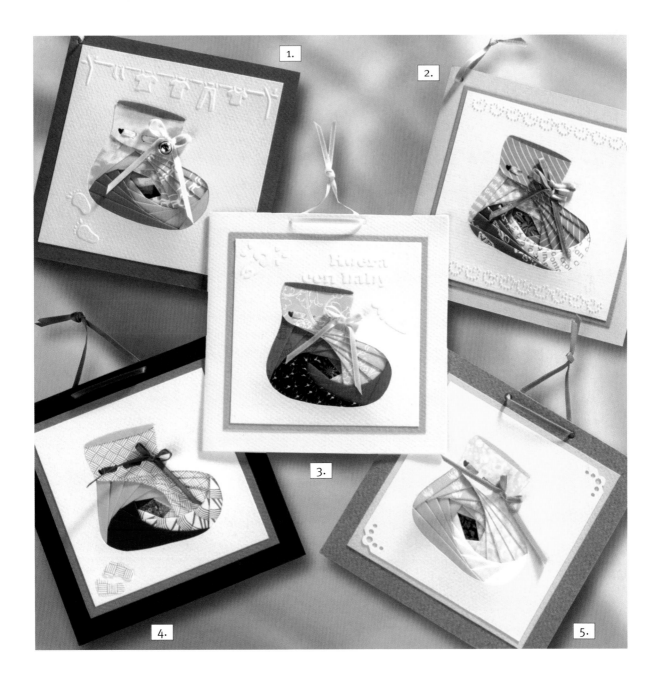

Socks

For the cutest baby.

All the socks are made according to the description given for card 1.

Card 1

Card: Havana brown C502 (13 x 26 cm) and dark pink C350 (11.6 x 11.6 cm) • Pattern 12 • 2 cm wide strips from 4 different yellow and brown envelopes • 3 x 5 cm envelope paper (colour D) • Gold deco

tape • Hole punch • Small heart hand punch • Feet and washing line embossing stencils • 30 cm cream ribbon • Copper coloured bell

Emboss the washing line and the feet in the small card. Only cut out the foot part of the sock from the small card. Use a light box to draw the leg (B) on the back of the piece of envelope paper (colour D) and cut it out. Use photo glue to stick it on the front of the card so that it joins the hole of the foot. Wait until the glue is dry and then punch out the hearts as shown in the diagram. After the IRIS folding, thread the ribbon through the hearts and tie it in a bow. Cut the small oval out of envelope paper (colour A) and stick it on the top of part B. Tie the bell onto the ribbon using a piece of cotton. Punch a hole in the top left-hand corner and make an eye through which to hang the card up using the rest of the ribbon.

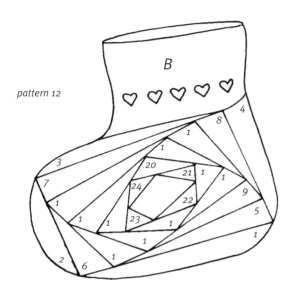

pattern 12

Card 2

Card: azure P04 (13 x 26 cm), turquoise P32 (11.3 x 11.3 cm) and pastel green A331 (10.7 x 10.7 cm) • Pattern 12 • 2 cm wide strips from 4 different green, aqua and white envelopes • 3 x 5 cm envelope paper (colour C) • oval (colour A) • Silver holographic paper • Hole punch • Small heart hand punch • Ornare baby decorative pricking template • 30 cm aqua-coloured ribbon
Prick a chicken border along the top and bottom of the smallest card.

Card 3

Card: light pink C103 (13 x 26 cm) • pink C352 (11 x 11 cm) and lily-white C110 (10.3 x 10.3 cm) • Pattern 12 • 2 cm wide strips from 4 different pink, red and purple envelopes • 3 x 5 cm envelope paper (colour C) • Oval (colour A) • Silver deco tape • Hole punch • Small heart hand punch • Baby embossing stencil • 30 cm pink ribbon
Emboss the white card.

Card 4

Card: indigo blue C140 (13 x 26 cm), turquoise C595 (11 x 11 cm) and lily-white C110 (10 x 10 cm) • Pattern 12 • 2 cm wide strips from 4 different blue envelopes from, for example, a government ministry and a school • 3 x 5 cm envelope paper (colour C) • oval (colour A) • Silver deco tape • Hole punch • Small heart hand punch • Foot punch • 30 cm blue ribbon
Punch out the feet. Punch two holes in the front of the dark card for the loop.

Card 5

Card: grey C431 (13 x 26 cm), butter yellow C400 (11 x 11 cm) and lemon yellow C101 (10.3 x 10.3 cm) • Pattern 12 • 2 cm wide strips from 4 different yellow, grey and white envelopes from, for example, the World Wildlife Fund and a university • 3 x 5 cm envelope (colour C) • oval (colour A) • Rainbow holographic paper • Hole punch • Small heart hand punch • Multi-corner punch • 30 cm light orange ribbon
Punch out two corners of the smallest card.

Hearts

Card 1

Card: light pink C103 (14.8 x 21 cm), cerise P33 (14 x 9.7 cm) and lavender blue C150 (13.8 x 9.4 cm) • Pattern13 • 2 cm strips from 3 blue, grey and red envelopes • Silver deco tape • Heart corner punch
Punch out the corners of the blue card and cut out the heart. IRIS fold the card with the strips.

Card 2

Card: pink A481 (14.8 x 21 cm) • pink C352 (11 x 9.7 cm) and light pink C103 (10 x 9 cm) • Pattern 13 • 2 cm wide strips from 3 different lilac and purple envelopes from, for example, a housing corporation • Silver deco tape • Multi-corner punch
Punch out two corners from the smallest card and cut out the heart at an angle.

Card 3

Card: violet C502 (14.8 x 21 cm) and shell white C112 (13.7 x 9.4 cm) • Pattern 13 • 2 cm wide strips from 3 different blue and purple envelopes from, for example, a hospital • Silver holographic paper • Multi-corner punch • Blue gel pen
After the IRIS folding, punch out four hearts from envelope paper and stick them in the corners of the white card. Draw blue lines to connect the hearts.

Card 4

Card: pink C352 (14.8 x 21 cm), grey C131 (13.5 x 9.9 cm) and light pink C103 (11.5 x 9.5 cm) • Pattern 13 • 2 cm wide strips from 3 different lilac and pink envelopes • Copper red deco tape • Heart corner punch
Punch out two corners from the smallest card.

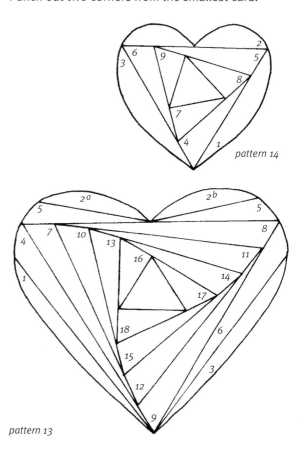

pattern 14

pattern 13

Card 5

*Card: red C505 (14.8 x 21 cm) and white A211
(12.8 x 9.5 cm) • Pattern 13 • 2 cm wide strips
from 3 different orange, red and purple envelopes
• Gold holographic paper • Regal corner punch
• Ornamental embossing stencil*
Cut the corners and cut the heart from the white
card. Emboss the red card in the cut-off corners.

Card 6

*Card: shell white C112 (14.8 x 21 cm) and red C505
(13.7 x 9.4 cm) • 2 cm wide strips from 3 different
white, yellow and orange envelopes • Gold
holographic paper • Small heart hand punch*
Cut the heart out of the red card and punch out the
small hearts.

Cherries and shells

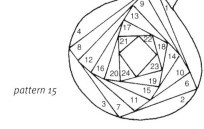

pattern 15

*IRIS folding without folding is called IRISING!
Take the attractively coloured Tissu strips and
fill the shells and cherries from the outside to
the inside following the numbers. All the cards
are made according to the instructions given
for card 1.*

Card 1

*Card: honey yellow A243 (14.8 x 21 cm), gold
mother-of-pearl P141 (14.3 x 10 cm) and white C335
(13.7 x 9.4 cm) • Pattern 15 • 5 mm wide Tissu strips
- light yellow, light beige, dark yellow and dark
beige • Gold deco tape • IRIS folding text sticker •
Border ornament punch (rope)*

1. Use a light box to copy the outline of the shell
   twice on the back of the white card.
2. Cut the shells out and punch the border.
3. Tape the pattern to the cutting mat.
4. Place the card on the pattern with one opening
   exactly over the pattern (you should be looking
   at the back of the card) and tape the left-hand
   side to the cutting mat using masking tape.
5. Lay out the strips ready to be used.
6. Take a strip of dark yellow paper and use it to
   cover section a, placing it exactly against the line
   of the pattern. Allow the other sides to protrude
   slightly. Cut the rest off.
7. Stick the left-hand and right-hand sides of the
   strip to the card using adhesive tape.

8. Next, cover section b using a dark yellow strip.
9. Take a light yellow strip, place it on section 1 of
   the pattern and cut off the excess. Tape the strip
   to the left and right-hand sides of the card.
10. Take a light beige strip. Place this on section 2
    and stick it into place.
11. Take a dark yellow strip. Place this on section 3
    and stick it into place.
12. Take a dark beige strip. Place this on section 4
    and stick it into place.
13. You have now gone all the way around. Start again
    with a light yellow strip on section 5, a light beige
    strip on section 6, a dark yellow strip on section 7
    and a dark beige strip on section 8. Continue
    going around the pattern. The strips on sections 1,
    5, 9, 13, 17 and 21 of this pattern are all light
    yellow. The strips on sections 2, 6, 10, 14, 18 and
    22 are all light beige. The strips on sections 3, 7,
    11, 15, 19 and 23 are all dark yellow. The strips on
    sections 4, 8, 12, 16, 20 and 24 are all dark beige.
14. Remove the card, place the second opening on
    the pattern and fill it with strips in the same way
    as before.
15. Finish the card as described for the basic circle
    and then stick it first on a mother-of-pearl card
    followed by a double card.

Card 2

Card: light brown C374 (13 x 6 cm), aquamarine P187 (12.1 x 12.1 cm), aquamarine P17 (11.8 x 11.8 cm) and maize C470 (11.1 x 11.1 cm) • Pattern 15 • 5 mm wide Tissu strips - 3 different shades of blue and soft green • Silver holographic paper • Punch (sea horse)

Card 3

Card: pastel green A331 (14.8 x 21 cm), cloudy beige P68 (13.1 x 9.8 cm) and white C335 (12.5 x 8.2 cm) • Pattern 15 • 5 mm wide Tissu strips - blue, green and beige • 3 mm wide pale blue Tissu strip for the border • Silver holographic paper • Flower corner punch

Card 4

Card: red A517 (14.8 x 21 cm) and white A211 (13.8 x 9.5 cm) • Pattern 16 • 5 mm wide Tissu strips - red, orange, beige, pale yellow and black • Gold deco tape • IRIS folding text sticker • 3-in-1 corner punch (Leaves)

Punch out the top corners of the white card and cut the cherries out of the back. Cut some narrow strips of black Tissu paper for the stalks. Stick them on the card after finishing the IRISING.

Card 5

Card: dark green A309 (14.8 x 21 cm), bright yellow C400 (13.5 x 9.1 cm) and white C335 (13.5 x 8.9 cm) • Pattern 16 • 5 mm wide Tissu strips - red, orange, 2 shades of yellow • Red holographic paper • Border ornament punch (Spring)

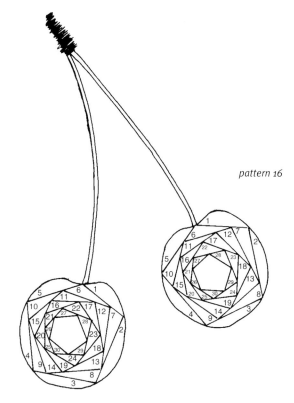

pattern 16

Card 6

Card: dark green A309 (14.8 x 21 cm), pastel green A331 (14 x 9.5 cm) and white C335 (13.5 x 9.1 cm) • Pattern 16 • 5 mm wide Tissu strips - 2 different shades of green and red • Silver holographic paper • IRIS folding sticker • Flower mosaic punch

Card 7

Card: red A517 (14.8 x 21 cm), mango A575 (13.9 x 9.5 cm) and white C335 (13.2 x 9.4 cm) • Pattern 16 • 5 mm wide Tissu strips - red, dark green and orange • Silver holographic paper • Heart border ornament punch

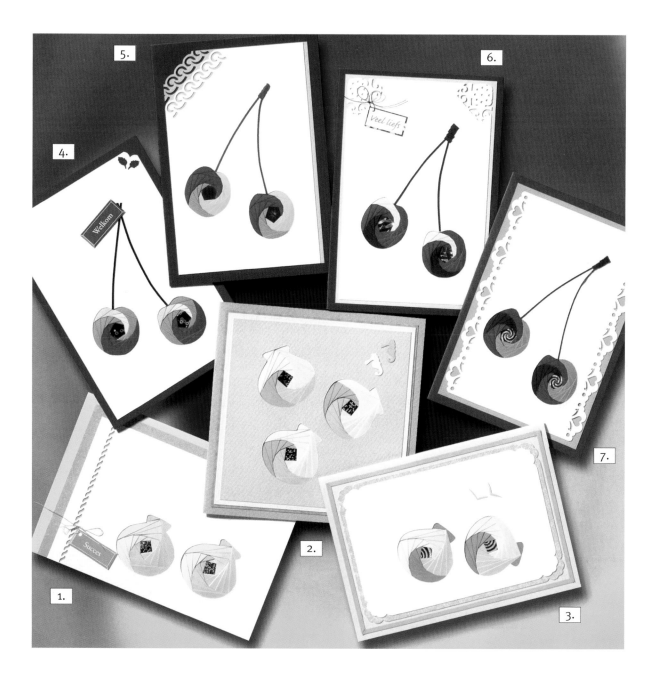

Squares

Make these square cards according to the instructions given for the basic square.

Card 1

Card: Christmas red P43 (14.8 x 21 cm), olive green P45 (13.5 x 9.5 cm) and carnation white P03 (12.2 x 9 cm) • Pattern 1 • 3 cm wide strips from 4 different red and beige envelopes • Bronze gel pen

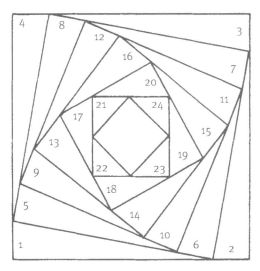

pattern 1

• Bronze-green embroidery silk • Bronze holographic paper
Thread the embroidery silk around the square.

Card 2

Card: green (14.8 x 21 cm), light green (13.9 x 10 cm) and white (12.3 x 9.7 cm) • Pattern 1 • 3 cm wide strips from 4 different green envelopes • Holly corner punch • Gold holographic paper
Punch out the two top corners.

Card 3

Card: white (14.8 x 21 cm and 14.6 x 10.3 cm) • Pattern 1 • 3 cm wide strips from 4 different beige and brown envelopes • Gold holographic paper with stars • Gold thread
Attach the gold thread using photo glue.

Card 4

Card: natural (14.8 x 21 cm) and yellow rainbow paper (13.8 x 9.5 cm) • Pattern 1 • 3 cm wide strips from 4 different yellow and beige envelopes • Diamond corner punch • Gold holographic paper
Cut the square out of the rainbow card. Punch out the corners and connect the corners using bronze lines.

Card 5

Card: white (14.8 x 21 cm and 14.6 x 10.3 cm) • Pattern 1 • 3 cm wide strips from 4 different red envelopes • Red holographic paper

Draw the half bow, fold it double along the dotted line and cut it out.

Card 6

Card: Christmas red P43 (14.8 x 21 cm) and white (14.2 x 9.9 cm) • Pattern 1 • 3 cm wide strips from 3 different red and green envelopes • Green "Merry Christmas" text strips • Gold holographic paper with stars

Finish this card with a box (3 x 4 cm) cut out of envelope paper. Attach the text strip's label using cotton.

Make accompanying labels with pattern 2.

half a bow

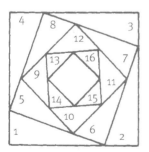

pattern 2

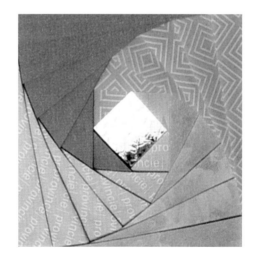

1.

2.

3.

4.

5.

6.

Playing with squares

Glued stars and

ice-crystals.

General information
The points for the star and the ice-crystal are made the same size by drawing a point on a wide strip of paper. Next, fold the strip double twice like a harmonica, staple it together and then cut out this point through the four layers. Cards 1, 3, 4 and 6: point a; card 5: points b and c; cards 2 and 7: point d.

Card 1
Card: violet P20 (14.8 x 21 cm and 14.6 x 10.3 cm)
• Pattern 1 • 3 cm wide strips from 4 different blue envelopes • Silver holographic paper
Fold the card double and open it again. Draw pencil lines on the left-hand inner half through the middle. Place pattern 1 over the lines and prick all four holes. Cut out the square and finish the card off according to the instructions given in the basic techniques.

Card 2
Card: violet P20 (13.3 x 26.6 cm) and white (11.9 x 11.9 cm) • Pattern 3 • 2 cm wide strips from 4 different blue envelopes • Silver holographic paper • Star corner punch • Dark blue gel pen
Punch out the corners of the white card. Cut a 12 x 5 cm strip of holographic paper and make the ice-crystal points. Decorate with lines using the gel pen.

Card 3
Card: iris blue P31 (14.8 x 21 cm and 14.6 x 10.3 cm)
• Pattern 1 • 3 cm wide strips from 4 different used blue and grey envelopes • Silver holographic paper
• Star punch

Card 4
Card: white P30 (14.8 x 21 cm and 14.6 x 10.3 cm)
• Pattern 1 • 3 cm wide strips from 3 different lilac and red envelopes • White and blue text strips •
Silver holographic paper • Silver gel pen

Card 5
Card: lilac P14 (13.3 x 26.6 cm) and lavender P21 (12.8 x 12.8 cm) • Pattern 3 • 2 cm wide strips from 3 different plain blue envelopes • Blue text strips • Silver holographic paper with stars • Geometric embossing stencil (Avec)
First, emboss the corners using the template's inner square. Cut the holographic paper to a size of 10 x 5 cm and 10 x 3.5 cm for the big and small points.

Card 6
Card: white (14.8 x 21 cm and 14.6 x 10.3 cm)
• Pattern 1 • 3 cm wide strips from 2 red and 2 grey used envelopes • Silver holographic paper
• Geometric embossing stencil

First, emboss the corners and cut the holographic paper to a size of 10 x 4 cm for the points.

Card 7

Card: lavender P21 (13.3 x 26.6 cm) and iris blue P31 (12.3 x 12.3 cm) • Pattern 3 • 2 cm wide strips from 4 different grey used envelopes • Silver holographic paper • Star corner punch • Star punch

First, punch out the corners of the iris blue card. Cut a 12 x 5 cm strip of holographic paper for the points.

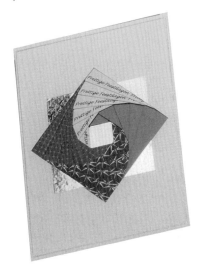

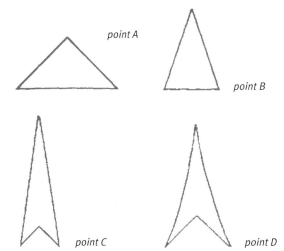

point A

point B

point C

point D

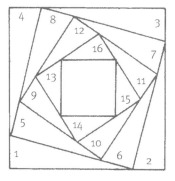

pattern 3

Candles

Creating light in

the dark winter months.

Card 1

Card: Christmas green P18 (14.8 x 21 cm and 14 x 9.7 cm) and white (14.4 x 10.1 cm) • Pattern 4 with flame A • 3 cm wide strips from 3 different green envelopes • Green text strips • Gold holographic paper • Sticker lines and stars

Copy the pattern onto the back of the white card and cut out the candle and the flame. Fill the hole of the candle with strips of envelope paper. Fill the flame with strips of holographic paper. Cut a 12.5 x 7.8 cm square out of the front of the green card. Stick the white card on the inside against the square using double-sided adhesive tape. Cover it with the green card.

Card 2

Card: night blue P41 (14.8 x 21 cm), iris blue P31 (13.3 x 9.5 cm) and white (13.5 x 9.1 cm) • Pattern 4 with flame B • 3 cm wide strips from 3 different blue envelopes • Blue text strips • Silver holographic paper with stars • Ornamental corner punch

Card 3

Card: Christmas red P43 (14.8 x 21 cm) and white (13.7 x 9 cm) • Pattern 4 with flame A •

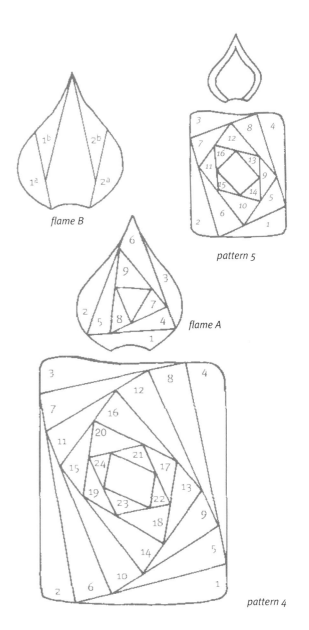

flame B

pattern 5

flame A

pattern 4

3 cm wide strips from 4 different grey and red envelopes • Silver holographic paper • Star corner punch

Card 1a

Card: carnation white P03 (7 x 11 cm, and 6.8 x 5.3 cm) • Pattern 5 • 2 cm wide strips from 4 different red envelopes • Red holographic paper • Ice-crystal from a corner punch
Only cut out the candle. Fill the hole with strips.
Cut the flame out of envelope paper and holographic paper. Stick the flame above the candle.
Tip: try using deco tape for the flame.

Card 2a

Card: white (7 x 11 cm, and 6.8 x 5.3 cm) • Pattern 5
• 2 cm wide strips from 4 different blue envelopes
• Silver holographic paper with stars • Blue gel pen

Card 3a

Card: Christmas red P43 (7 x 11 cm, and 6.8 x 5.3 cm) • Pattern 5 • 2 cm wide strips from 4 different grey and red envelopes • Silver holographic paper • Silver gel pen

Christmas bells

To the left and right

Let them ring out!

Card 1

Card: night blue P41 (14.8 x 21 cm) and lavender P21 (13 x 9.2 cm) • Pattern 6 • 2.5 cm wide strips from 4 different blue envelopes • Silver holographic paper • Embossing stencil

Emboss the text on the lavender card. Cut out the shape (note: not the tongue or the suspension eye!). Finish the card as described in the basic technique. Cut out the tongue and the suspension eye from envelope paper and stick them onto the card.

Card 2

Card: Christmas red P43 (14.8 x 21 cm) • Silver holographic paper (14.1 x 10.1 cm) and iris blue holographic paper no. 31 (13.7 x 9.8 cm) • Pattern 7 • 2.5 cm wide strips from 3 different light blue envelopes • White and blue text strips • Silver holographic paper • Comet embossing stencil • Star punch

First, emboss (see page 11) the comet and 2 stars, and then stick the punched out white stars on the card.

Card 3

Card: carnation white P03 (14.8 x 21 cm) and violet P20 (11.6 x 7.9 cm) • Pattern 7 • 2.5 cm wide strips

from 4 different blue envelopes • Silver holographic paper • Holly embossing stencil

Emboss the top right-hand corner of the white card. Round off the top right-hand corner of the violet card.

Card 4

*Card: night blue P41 (14.8 x 21 cm)
and carnation white P03 (13.8 x
9.5 cm) • Pattern 7 • 2.5 cm wide
strips from 4 different used blue
envelopes • Silver holographic
paper with stars • Silver gel pen
• Holly corner punch*

Card 5

*Card: carnation white
P03 (14.8 x 21 cm),
iris blue no. 31
(12.3 x 9.6 cm) and
lavender P21 (10.5 x
8.7 cm) • Pattern 6 •
2.5 cm wide strips from 4 blue different envelopes • Silver holographic
paper • Text sticker • Star punch*
Round off the corners of all the cards.

Card 6

*Card: night blue P41 (14.8 x 21 cm), silver
holographic paper (14.2 x 10 cm) and carnation
white P03 (13.8 x 9.5 cm) • Pattern 6 • 2.5 cm
wide strips from 3 different blue envelopes •
Blue text strips • Silver holographic paper
• Star corner punch*
Punch out the corners of the white card.

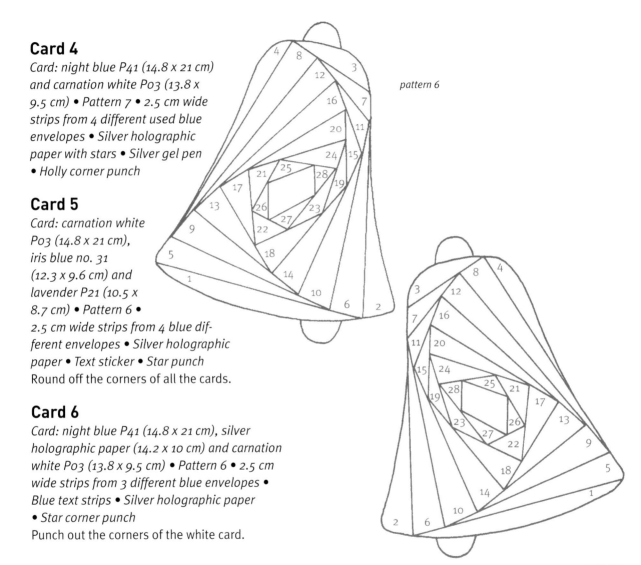

pattern 6

pattern 7

1. 2. 3. 4. 5. 6.

Christmas balls

It isn't Christmas without these decorations!

Card 1

Card: Christmas red P43 (13.3 x 26.6 cm) and white (11.8 x 11.8 cm) • Pattern 8 • 3 cm wide strips from 2 red and 3 grey envelopes • Silver holographic paper • Holly corner punch

Punch out the corners of the white card. Cut out the Ø 7.5 cm circle slightly below the centre point (because of the suspension eye). Fill the ball according to the pattern. Copy the shape of the half suspension eye (see page 81) onto the holographic paper. Next, fold it double over the dotted line. Cut it out and stick it above the Christmas ball.

Card 2

Card: Christmas green P18 (13.3 x 26.6 cm) and white (10.7 x 10.7 cm) • Pattern 8 • 3 cm wide strips from 5 different green envelopes • Silver holographic paper for the small strips and the middle • Shell figure scissors

Cut decorative borders around the white card. Cut out the Ø 7.5 cm circle slightly below the middle point. Cut out 1 cm wide strips from the holographic paper. To make a nice fold line, score the back using a ruler and a pin. Add these small strips to colour B for sections 2, 7, 12, etc. This means that you must place a strip of colour B against the dotted line of

section 2 and stick it in place. Place a small strip of holographic paper over the top of it against the continuous line of section 2 and stick it in place. Continue with the other colours in sections 3, 4, 5 and 6. For section 7, place another strip of colour B against the dotted line and then place another small strip of holographic paper against the continuous line, etc. At the end, stick the finished design on the double green card. Make a suspension eye as described for card 1.

Card 3

Card: dark green (13.3 x 26.6 cm and 11.2 x 11.2) and white (12.6 x 12.6 cm) • Pattern 8 • 3 cm wide strips from 4 different aquamarine envelopes • Gold holographic paper • Green text strips

Cut out the Ø 7.5 cm circle slightly below the centre of the white card. Cut out 1 cm wide strips from gold holographic paper and add them to colour E in sections 5, 10, 15, etc. as described for card 2. Make a suspension eye as described for card 1 and stick it above the Christmas ball together with a small gold ribbon. Cut a 10.6 x 10.6 cm square out of the front of the green card. Stick the white card behind it using double-sided adhesive tape. Cover the back of the design with the small green card.

Card 4

Card: Christmas red P43 (13.3 x 26.6 cm) and white (12.4 x 12.4 cm) • Pattern 8 • 3 cm wide strips from 5 different red envelopes • Gold holographic paper • Geometric embossing stencil
Copy the corners of the embossing stencil onto the back of the white card using a pencil. Cut out the corners. Cut 1 cm wide strips from holographic paper and add these to colour B in sections 2, 7, 12, etc. Use a real hook or cut one out of holographic paper.

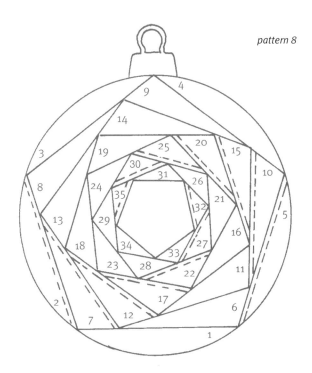

pattern 8

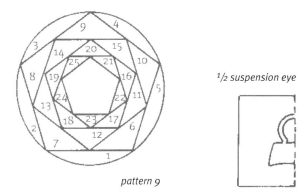

pattern 9

½ suspension eye

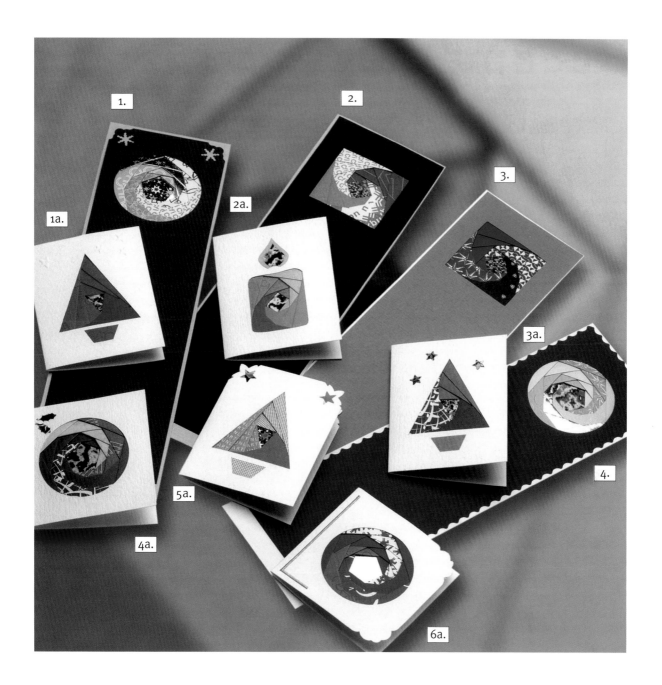

Bookmarkers and labels

Bookmarker 1
Card: lavender P21 (21 x 6 cm) and Christmas green P18 (20 x 5.6 cm) • Pattern 9 • 1.5 cm wide strips from 5 different grey envelopes • Silver holographic paper • Ice-crystal corner punch

Bookmarker 2
Card: lavender P21 (21 x 6 cm) and night blue P41 (20 x 5.7 cm) • Pattern 2 • 2 cm wide strips from scrap pieces of grey and red envelopes • Silver holographic paper

Bookmarker 3
Card: snow-white P30 (21 x 6 cm) and violet P20 (20 x 5.7 cm) • Pattern 2 • 2 cm wide strips from scrap pieces of blue envelopes • Silver holographic paper

Bookmarker 4
Card: carnation white P03 (21 x 6 cm) and Christmas red P43 (20 x 6 cm) • Pattern 9 • 1.5 cm wide strips from 5 different beige envelopes • Gold holographic paper • Shell figure scissors

Card 1a
Card: white (7 x 11 cm and 6.8 x 5.3 cm) • Pattern 10 • 2 cm wide strips from scrap pieces of 3 different red envelopes • Red holographic paper • Star embossing stencil
Only cut out the tree. Stick the pot underneath at the end.

Card 2a
Card: white (7 x 11 cm) and yellow (6.8 x 5.3 cm) • Pattern 5 • 2 cm wide strips from 4 different red, orange and yellow envelopes • Gold holographic paper

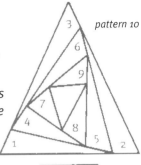
pattern 10

Card 3a
Card: white (7 x 11 cm and 6.8 x 5.3 cm) • Pattern 10 • 2 cm wide strips from scrap pieces of 3 different green envelopes • Gold holographic paper • Star punch

Card 4a
Card: white (6 x 12 cm and 5.8 x 5.8 cm) • Pattern 9 • 1.5 cm wide strips from scrap pieces of 5 different green envelopes • Gold holographic paper • Holly corner punch

Card 5a
Card: white (7 x 11 cm and 6.8 x 5.3 cm) • Pattern 10 • 2 cm wide strips from scrap pieces of 3 different blue envelopes • Silver holographic paper • Star corner punch

Card 6a
Card: white (6 x 12 cm and 5.8 x 5.8 cm) • Pattern 9 • 1.5 cm wide strips from scrap pieces of 5 different red envelopes • Gold holographic paper • Flower corner punch • Red and gold gel pens

Champagne glasses

Cheers and best wishes

for the New Year!

Card 1

Card: night blue P41 (21 x 10.5 cm), caramel P26 (19.3 x 9.8 cm) and carnation white P03 (18.9 x 9.4 cm) • Pattern 11 • 2.5 cm wide strips from 4 different yellow, beige and green envelopes • 1 cm wide strips of gold holographic paper • Gold holographic paper • Hole punch

Cut out the tops of the glasses from the white card and fill them with strips. Note: add the narrow strips

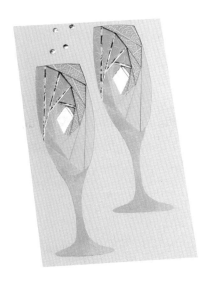

of holographic paper to colour D as follows. Cover section 1 with strips of colour A, section 2 with strips of colour B and section 3 with strips of colour C. Next, place a strip of colour D against the dotted line of section 4 and stick it in place. Place a narrow strip of holographic paper over this against the continuous line of section 4 (see Christmas balls, card 2). Continue round and add a narrow strip of holographic paper in sections 8, 12, etc. Cut out two stems at the same time from a piece of double-folded envelope paper and stick these on the card.

Card 2

Card: carnation white P03 (21 x 10.5 cm) and wine red P36 (19.3 x 9.7 cm) • Pattern 11 • 2.5 cm wide strips from 4 different beige and yellow envelopes • 1 cm wide strips of gold holographic paper • Gold holographic paper • Hole punch
Cut out the tops of the glasses from the wine red card. Note: add the narrow strips of holographic paper to colour B in sections 2, 6, 10, etc. according to the instructions given for card 1.

Card 3

Card: nut brown P39 (21 x 10.5 cm) and carnation white P03 (19.1 x 9.5 cm) • Pattern 11 • 2.5 cm wide strips from 4 different grey, beige and yellow envelopes • 1 cm wide strips of gold holographic paper • Gold holographic paper • Bronze gel pen • Hole punch
Add the strips of holographic paper to colour B in sections 2, 6, 10, etc. according to the instructions given for card 1.

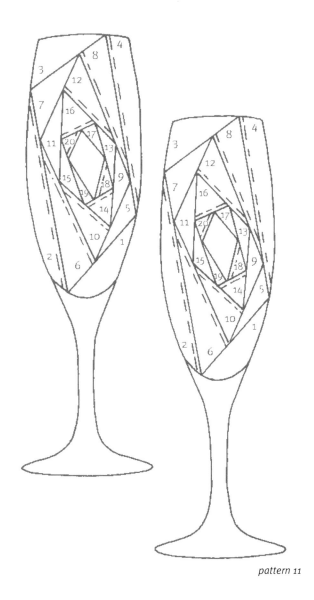

pattern 11

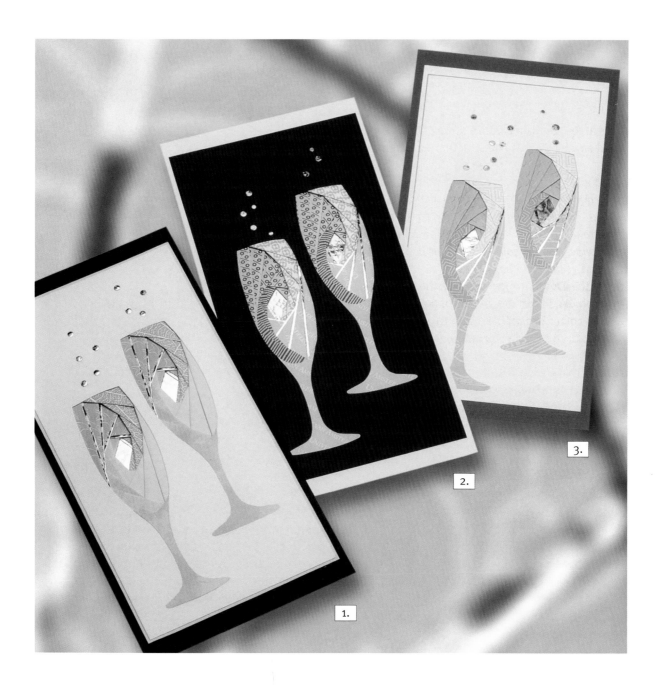

1.

2.

3.

Christmas tree and double star

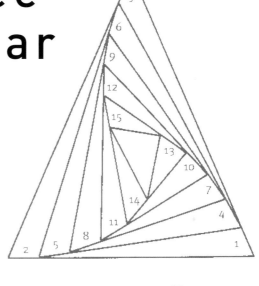

What would a Christmas card

be without a Christmas tree?

Card 1

Card: carnation white P03 (14.8 x 21 cm), red (13.8 x 9.5 cm) and raven black P01 (13. x 8.7 cm) • Pattern 12 • 2 cm wide strips from 2 grey envelopes and 1 white envelope • Silver holographic paper • Star corner punch

First, cut out a 3 mm strip from both sides of the red card and stick it on the card with a 1 mm gap to the left and to the right of the red card.

Card 2

Card: dark green (14.8 x 21 cm), gold (13.6 x 9.7 cm) and white (13.2 x 9.2 cm) • Pattern 12 • 2 cm wide strips from 2 different green envelopes • Green text strips

Card 3

Card: carnation white P03 (14.8 x 21 cm) and raven black P01 (13.8 x 9.5 cm) • Holographic card (14.1 x 9.8 cm) • Pattern 12 • 2 cm wide strips from 2 different blue envelopes • White with blue text strips • Star corner punch

Punch out the corners of the holographic card.

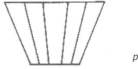

pattern 12

Punch out the corners of the black card and cut the stars out.

Card 4

Card: white P30 (14.8 x 21 cm), gold (14.8 x 10.5 cm) and green P18 (14.8 x 9.3 cm) • Pattern 12 • 2 cm wide strips from 2 different green envelopes • White with green text strips • Gold holographic paper • Ice-crystals from a corner punch • Shell figure scissors

Loose stars and ice-crystals punched out of deco tape are easy to stick on the card.

Card 5

Card: Christmas green P18 (14.8 x 21 cm), red (14.3 x 9.5 cm) and white (13.3 x 8.5 cm) • Pattern 12 • 2 cm wide strips from 3 different red envelopes • Silver holographic paper • Silhouette stars embossing stencil (Linda Design)

Card 6

Card: lavender P21 (13.3 x 26.6 cm) and iris blue P31 (12.2 x 12.2 cm) • Pattern 13 • 2 cm wide strips from 3 different grey and blue envelopes • 1 cm wide strips of holographic paper • Silver holographic paper • Star corner punch • Star hand punch
Cut out the star from the smallest card. Add the narrow strips of holographic paper to colour C. Place a strip of colour A on section 1 and a strip of colour B on section 2. Place a strip of colour C against the dotted line of section 3 and a narrow strip of holographic paper on top against the continuous line (see 'Christmas balls', card 2). Repeat this on sections 6, 9, 12, etc.

Card 7

Card: red (14.8 x 21 cm) and mother-of-pearl (13.4 x 9.6 cm) • Pattern 13 • 2 cm wide strips from 2 grey envelopes and 1 red envelope • Silver holographic paper • Geometric embossing stencil

Card 8

Card: mother-of-pearl (13.3 x 26.6 cm) and iris blue P31 (12.3 x 12.3 cm) • Pattern 13 • 2 cm wide strips
from 3 different grey envelopes • Silver holographic paper • Star corner punch

Card 9

Card: white (14.8 x 21 cm and 14.6 x 10.3 cm) • Pattern 13 • 2 cm wide strips from 3 different blue envelopes • 1 cm wide strips of silver holographic paper for colour B • Silver holographic paper • Holly embossing stencil
Add the narrow silver strips to colour B. Finish the card as described for card 6, but for sections 2, 5, 8, 11, etc.

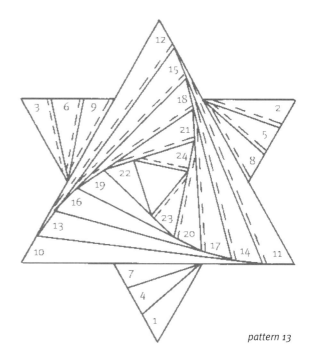

pattern 13

Woolly hat and jumper

Warmly dressed for winter.

Card 1

Card: purple P13 (14.8 x 21 cm) and white (12.5 x 8.6 cm) • Pattern 14 • 2.5 cm wide strips from orange, pink and purple envelopes • 2.5 x 8 cm strip of colour C • Gold holographic paper • Ice-crystal corner punch • Snow embossing stencil • Bobble

Cut the woolly hat out of the white card; be careful: do not cut the brim. Emboss the snowflakes. Fill the shape. For the brim of the woolly hat, put the wide strip through the ridge master, cut out the shape and stick it to the card. Punch out the ice-crystals. Finally, stick the bobble onto the card.

Card 2

Card: aquamarine (14.8 x 21 cm), night blue P41 (13.5 x 9.5 cm) and carnation white P03 (12.5 x 8.6 cm) • Pattern 14 • 2.5 cm wide strips from 3 different purple and aquamarine envelopes • 2.5 x 8 cm strip of colour B • Rainbow holographic paper • Ice-crystal punch • Bobble

Card 3

Card: dark blue P41 (14.8 x 21 cm), pink (13.1 x 9.6 cm) and mother-of-pearl (13.6 x 9.1 cm) • Pattern 15 • 3 cm wide strips from 4 different purple envelopes • Silver holographic paper • Star punch

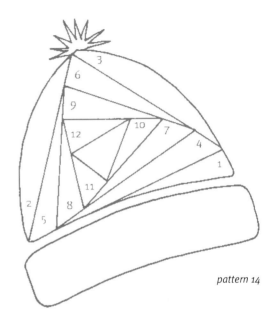

pattern 14

Cut the body (not the sleeves) out of the mother-of-pearl card. Fill the hole with the strips. Copy the sleeves of the pattern onto the back of envelope paper (colour C). Cut them out and stick them next to the jumper.

Card 4

Card: olive green P45 (14.8 x 21 cm), aquamarine (14.1 x 10.1 cm), night blue P41 (13.4 x 9.8 cm) and white (13.2 x 9.1 cm) • Pattern 15 • 3 cm wide strips from 3 different green envelopes • Green text strips • Silver holographic paper • Ice-crystals from the corner punch

Card 5

Card: turquoise P32 (14.8 x 21 cm), night blue P41 (14 x 9.6 cm) and white (12.7 x 9.3 cm) • Pattern 14 • 2.5 cm wide strips from 3 different bright green envelopes • 2.5 x 8 cm strip of colour C • Silver holographic paper • Ice-crystal figure punch • Bobble

Cut the woolly hat and punch out the ice-crystals from the white card.

Card 6

Card: night blue P41 (14.8 x 21 cm) and carnation white P03 (13.3 x 9.7 cm) • Pattern 14 • 2.5 cm wide strips from 3 different blue envelopes • 2.5 x 8 cm strip of colour C • Silver holographic paper • Star corner punch • Snow embossing stencil • Bobble

Card 7

Card: purple P13 (14.8 x 21 cm) and white (13.7 x 9.2 cm) • Pattern 15 • 3 cm wide strips from 4 different purple, orange and red envelopes • Gold holographic paper • Ice-crystal corner punch

Card 8

Card: white (14.8 x 21 cm and 14.6 x 10.3 cm) • Pattern 15 • 3 cm wide strips from 4 different blue envelopes • Silver holographic

paper • Figure scissors • Snow embossing stencil

Emboss the snowflakes (see page 11). Cut the body out of the 'landscape' card. Cut the sleeves from envelope paper (colour B). Cut a decorative border along the bottom edge. Fill the border with a strip which measures 2 x 14.8 cm (colour A). Cover the design.

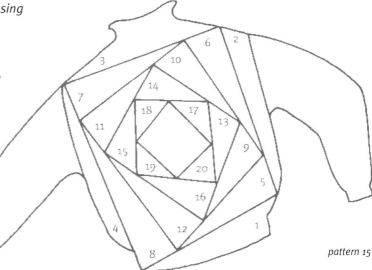

pattern 15

Cooking pears

Sweet wintertime fruit!

Card

Card: brick red C130 (14.8 x 21 cm), off-white C335 (7.5 x 5.4 cm), pear IRIS folding pattern (pattern 16), 4 envelopes ranging in colour from vanilla to burgundy, copper deco tape, vellum with a flower pattern (14.8 x 21 cm), text sticker

Copy the outline of the pear on the back of the white card. Cut the pear out, but not the stalk.

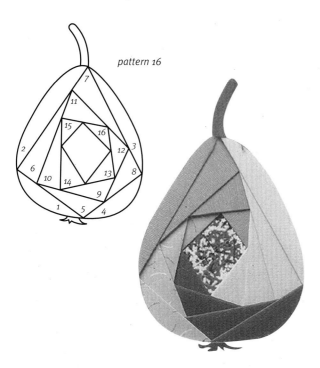

pattern 16

Stick pattern 16 and then the white card to your cutting mat. Cut the envelopes into 2 cm wide strips (lengthways or widthways) and sort them into colour A, colour B, colour C and colour D. Fold a border with is approximately 7 mm wide along the entire length of each strip making sure the nice side faces outwards. Do the IRIS folding according to the basic method. The strips on sections 1, 5, 9 and 13 of this pattern are all colour A. The strips on sections 2, 6, 10 and 14 are all colour B. The strips on sections 3, 7, 11 and 15 are all colour C. The strips on sections 4, 8, 12 and 16 are all colour D. Carefully remove the card after covering section 16. Stick a piece of gold deco tape to the back of the card, in the middle. Cut the deco tape into 8 mm strips and stick them on the white card to make a 4 mm wide frame. Cut the stalk out of envelope paper and stick it at the top of the pear. Fold the vellum around the card. Place the IRIS folding card on top of the vellum on the front of the card. Use a pencil to mark the four corners, approximately 3 mm away from the card. Carefully cut the frame out of the vellum using the cutting mat. Use two small pieces of double-sided adhesive tape to stick the vellum next to the fold at the back of the double card. Next, stick pieces of double-sided adhesive tape along the edges of the back of the IRIS folding card. Do not use glue, because all the strips place pressure on the card. Remove the protective layer and stick the card exactly in the middle of the double card. Finally hang the sticker on the stalk.

Our thanks go to

De Papieren Regenboog, Utrecht, the Netherlands (Papicolor card) for providing the materials.

Kars & Co BV, Ochten, the Netherlands

Koninklijke Talens, Apeldoorn, the Netherlands (card material)

CreaArt, Apeldoorn, the Netherlands for providing the material.

Nederlandse Vereniging voor Papierknipkunst (Dutch Society for Paper Cutting Art) for the cutting tips.
Info: http://home.hetnet.nl/~knipkunst or telephone: +31 (0) 548 54 13 23

The materials can be ordered by shopkeepers from:
Ecstasy Crafts, Shannonville, Canada
For a suppliers list in the UK please contact Search Press, Tunbridge Wells, United Kingdom